ISAAC PRESENTING REBECCA TO ABRAHAM

BIBLE STORIES

FOR

THE LITTLE ONES.

FROM

THE CREATION TO MOSES

BY THE AUTHOR OF

"EARNEST: A TRUE STORY," ETC.

NEW YORK

JAMES POTT & CO.

119-121 WEST 23D ST.

PREFACE.

In writing these Bible-stories for little children, in monosyllables, the language of the Bible has been adhered to as closely as possible. There is a sacredness in the very words of Holy Writ which children feel powerfully; and they will listen with much more attention to the Bible when it is read in church or in the family, if they hear the same words with which they are already familiar in their story-book.

It has been found impossible to avoid using a few two-syllable words, especially the words father, mother, sister and brother. The stories of the patriarchs are so exclusively annals of family life, that to leave out these family names, would destroy all life and interest in the narrative. They have accordingly been retained, as well as the word angel a few times, proper names, and numbers.

With these exceptions, the book is strictly monosyllabic.

CONTENTS.

FROM THE

CREATION TO MOSES.

Chapter I.

THE CREATION.

Who made this world and all things in it? the sky that is so blue and so bright, the sun that shines all day, and the moon and stars that shine all night, the grass that looks so green, the trees that are so high and shade us so well, and where the birds build their nests? Who made the plants to grow, the birds to sing, the cows, and dogs, and cats, and pigs, and hens, that I love to look at? Who made the boys and girls? Who made all things?

It was God. God was when all these things were not, and He made them all.

First He made the light. It was all dark, and the earth had no form, but God said, "Let there be light, and there was light." The light was good, and God did call it Day. This was the first day.

The next day God made the sky, and this was Heaven.

The third day, God made the sea and the dry land, and it was all good. He made the earth bring forth grass, and all plants, and in each plant He made its own seed, so that new plants might grow from it. The round earth was all full of grass and trees and plants in bloom, and all were so good. God was good to make them all. This was the Third Day.

On the Fourth Day God said, "Let there be lights in the sky, to make days, and nights, and months, and years." And God made two great lights—the sun to rule the day, and the moon to rule the night; He made the stars, too, and set them all in the sky, to give light on the earth. And God saw that it was good.

And God said, "Let the air be full of birds and fowl, and let the sea be full of fish." And he made great whales, and all the fish that swim in the sea and in the lakes and streams, and all the birds and fowls, great and small, that fly. And God saw that it was good, and He blest them. This was the Fifth Day.

And God said, " Let the earth bring forth all kinds of beasts," cows, and sheep, and dogs, and cats, and all wild beasts, and all small things like bees, and flies, and bugs, and snails, and worms.

And God said, " Let us make man like us, and let him rule the fish of the sea and the fowl of the air, and the beasts of the fields, and all the earth." So God made man out of the dust of the ground, and put in him the breath of life. He made man, and blest him, and said, " Take this earth and live in it and rule it, and all things that live on it. I give you to eat all herbs that have seed, on the face of the earth, and all trees in which is the fruit of a tree with its seed; to you they shall be for food. And to all beasts of the earth, and to all fowls of the air, and to all things that move on the earth that have life, I give all green herbs for meat." And it was so.

And God saw all things that He had made, and lo! it was all good. This was the Sixth Day.

So the sky and the earth were made and all things in them, and on the day next to the sixth day, God had rest from all His work which He had made, and He blest that day, for in it He did rest from all his His work which he had done.

God tells us to rest on that day as He did. I love God, for He made all this good world, and made me to live in it.

CHAPTER II.

EDEN.

GOD had made all things good, and last of all and best of all He had made man.

And the Lord God made a sweet place full of good things, the name of which was Eden, and there he put the man whom He had made. And out of the ground made the Lord God to grow all trees that are good to look at and good for food; with the tree of life in the midst, and a tree that would make one know good and bad things.

And the Lord God took the man and put him in Eden to dress it and to keep it. And He told the man, " Of all the trees you may eat, but of the tree that makes known good and bad you shall not eat; for in the day that you eat of it you shall die."

The man's name was Adam, and his wife's name was Eve. The Lord God brought all the beasts of the field and all the fowls of the air, and told Adam to give them names; and he gave each one its name.

So Adam and Eve dwelt in sweet Eden, and were full of love for God, and for all the good things that God had made for them. The birds sang in the trees, the plants were bright in their bloom, the sun shone, and the moon gave her light. The beasts were all tame, and did not hurt Adam and

Eve. God was with them both day and night, and all was love and joy and peace.

But Satan came to Eden in the form of a snake to tempt Adam and Eve. And he came to Eve first, and said, "Hath God said ye shall not eat of all the trees in Eden?"

And Eve said to him, "We may eat of the fruit of the trees, but of the fruit of the tree which is in the midst, the tree of good and bad, God hath said ye shall not eat of it, nor shall ye touch it, lest ye die."

Then Satan said to her, "Ye shall not die; for God doth know that in the day ye eat of it, ye shall be as gods, and know good and bad."

Oh, if Eve had but left Satan when he bade her do that which God had told her not to do. But she thought she would like to know what he would say next, and so she would talk with him; and then, when his talk was worse and worse, and she ought to have fled from him, she, too, had bad thoughts of God, and would try to get that which God had told her not to touch. So it is; if we stop to talk with sin and to find fault with God, we shall be sure to do some wrong act in the end. When Satan tempts us to sin, we must run from him, and drive the wrong thoughts out of our minds.

But Eve did not do so. She would look at the tree, and when she saw it was good for food, a nice tree, and she thought it would make her wise, she did what Satan told her to do, and what God had told her not to do. She took the fruit and did eat, and gave some to Adam, and he did eat.

But as soon as they had ate, they knew they had done wrong, and felt that it was sin to do what God had told them not to do. And when they heard the voice of the Lord God in the cool of the day, they were full of fear, and hid from Him in the trees.

And the Lord God spoke to Adam, and said to him, "Where art thou?"

And he said, "I heard thy voice, and was full of fear, and went and hid."

For the first time Adam did not dare to meet God's eye; for he had done wrong, and sin brings fear and shame with it.

God knows all things, and He knew what they had done; and He said to

Adam, "Didst thou eat of the tree that I told thee not to eat of?"

And the man said, "Eve, whom thou didst give me to be with me, gave me the fruit of the tree, and I did eat."

And the Lord God said to Eve, "What is this that thou hast done?"

And she said, "Satan told me to eat, and I did eat."

And the Lord God said to Satan, who was there in the form of a snake, "Since thou hast done this, thou art curst more than all the beasts of the field; thou shalt crawl on the ground and dust shalt thou eat all the days of thy life. Though thou wilt try to hurt man and make him do wrong, he shall at last tread thee down and bruise thy head; thou shalt not rule him, though thou wilt try hard to do so.

To Eve the Lord said, "Thou shalt oft be sad and sick, for thou hast done what I told thee not to do."

And to Adam He said, "Since thou didst eat of the tree of which I said to thee, thou shalt not eat of it, curst is the ground for thy sake; thorns and weeds shall it bring forth to thee. Thou shalt eat the herb of the field. In the sweat of thy face shalt thou work and eat bread, till thou art laid in the ground; for out of it wast thou made. Dust thou art, and to dust shalt thou turn."

Then God made coats of skins and put them on Adam and Eve; for, though they had left Him to serve Satan, He was still kind to them.

ADAM AND EVE DRIVEN OUT OF EDEN

And God said, "The man ate of the tree, and he knows good and bad, and now, lest he put forth his hand and take of the tree of life and live for all time," the Lord God sent him forth from Eden, to till the ground from which he was made. So He drove out the man, and put at the east of Eden a sword of fire, which should turn all ways, to keep the way of the tree of life.

Poor Adam and Eve! they could not live in Eden any more, for their sin was great, and they had done what God, the God who made them, had told them not to do. How sad they felt as they left their sweet home, and went out to work and toil in the earth.

But God still had love for them He gave them clothes and fed them;

He told them He would not let Satan rule them, but would one day give them a child who should put down Satan. That child was Jesus Christ, who was born to save man from sin and Satan.

So, though Adam and Eve had to leave Eden, they still had God to love them. If they tried to be good He would help them.

Chapter III.

CAIN AND ABEL.

Adam and Eve had two sons, Cain and Abel, and when they were grown up, Abel had to keep sheep and Cain to till the ground.

And it came to pass that Cain brought some of the fruit of the ground to give to the Lord. And Abel brought some lambs of his flock.

And the Lord had love for Abel and his gift, but Cain and his gift did not please him ; for He had told them to bring to Him lambs and not fruits.

When Cain saw that God had love

for Abel and not for him, he was very wroth, and his looks were dark and bad.

And the Lord said to Cain, "Why art thou wroth, and why is thy face so sad? If thou wilt be good, shall I not love thee? And if thou wilt not do right, it is thine own fault."

Was not God kind, thus to try to bring back Cain to be good? Yet Cain was still bad. He was too bad to heed God's words. He met Abel, and it came to pass that when they were in the field, he rose up and slew him.

How sad this was! Why did Cain want to kill Abel? He felt that he was bad and Abel was good, and so he slew him. And now he must pay for his crime all his life long.

The Lord said to Cain, "Where is Abel?"

And he said, "I know not. I do not take care of him."

Thus Cain told a lie to hide his sin. But how vain to try to hide it from God, who sees all that is done on the earth!

And God said, "What hast thou done? I know that thou hast slain him. And now thou art curst; thou shalt go up and down on the earth; when thou shalt work, the ground shall not yield her fruit to thee, for thou hast shed thy brother's blood."

And Cain said to the Lord, "I can not bear this. Thou hast sent me out this day from the face of the earth, and from thy face shall I be hid. And I shall go up and down in the earth, and it shall come to pass that all that find me will kill me."

And the Lord said to Cain, "No one shall kill thee;" and the Lord set a mark on Cain, so that no one might kill him.

How much sin and pain did Cain's wrath bring on him and on his father and mother. How sad it is to see a man or boy hate his brother! When we feel hate in our hearts, let us take care and drive it right out, for it was hate that made Cain kill Abel.

CHAPTER IV.

NOAH'S ARK.

THE world grew more and more full of men; but they were all bad; there was none that did good. Men, too, grew to be old; each man got to be six or eight times as old as men are now, and they were tall and large, and of great size.

God saw that men were bad, and that they did not love or serve Him at all. How strange that they should so soon leave God, and make a bad use of all His good gifts!

When the Lord saw how bad men were, He was sad that he had made them on the earth, and grief was in His heart. And He said, "I will take man from the face of the earth; both man and beast and the fowls of the air; for I grieve that I have made them."

But there was one good man, whose name was Noah, and who found grace in the eyes of the Lord. Noah was a just man, and his walk was with God. He had three sons, Shem, Ham and Japheth.

And God said to Noah, "The end of all flesh is at hand; for the earth is full of sin through them, and lo! I will take them from the earth.

"Make thee an ark of wood; rooms shalt thou make in the ark, and shalt pitch it on all sides with pitch."

Then God told Noah just how to

make the ark; how long and how wide it must be. And He said, "Thou shalt make a place in the roof to look out of, and thou shalt set the door in the side of it; and three floors high shalt thou make it.

For I will bring a flood of rain on the earth, to kill all flesh that has the breath of life; and all things that are on the earth shall die. But thee I will spare, and thou shalt come in the ark, thou and thy wife, and thy sons and thy sons' wives with thee. And of all beasts, two of each sort shall thou bring in the ark, to save them with thee. And take food of all kinds for thee and for the beasts to eat."

Thus did Noah: all that God told him he did; for he had faith, and knew that what God said would come to pass; and so, though the sky was calm and the earth fair and green, and though all things went on just as they had done, still Noah got the wood and built the ark to save him from the flood that he knew would come. He saw the men round him buy and sell, and plant and build, just as though there would be no flood. He told them to be good, and to flee from the wrath to to come, but they would mock at him, and would not think of God or care for Him. They all went their own way till the day that the flood came, and it was too late to turn to God.

God tells us in His Word that He will burn this earth with fire at the last day, as He sent the great flood in the days of Noah. Then Christ will come to judge the world, and He will save the good, but the bad he will not save. He tells us to be good, and watch for that day when He will come, and then we shall be glad to see Him, for He will take us to the skies to live in joy with Him; but if we do not think of Christ, or try to be good for His sake, we shall be full of fear when He comes, just as those men were who did not care for God when the flood came.

At last, when the ark was all done, God said to Noah: "Come, thou and all thy house, in the ark; for thou dost love me, and hast done as I have bade thee. Bring the beasts, two of each sort, with thee, and come. For in one week I will cause it to rain on the earth two score days and nights; and all things that live, that I have made on the face of the earth, shall die."

And Noah did as God told him. He was six hundred years old when he went in the ark. Two and two of all beasts went in the ark with Noah. And the Lord shut him in.

And in one week the springs of the great deep broke up, the sea came on the land, and the rain came down from the skies. And the rain was on the earth two score days and two score nights. The sea rose and bore up the ark, and the ark did float on the face of the deep. Then the sea rose more and more, till it beat on the tops of .he high hills. These, too, sank, and no more land was to be seen. All died that were on the earth; men, and beasts, and fowls; all were gone. All save Noah and they that were with him in the ark; and for five whole months the ark rode on the sea, lone and drear. But it was not lost, for God took care of it.

God thought of Noah and of all the beasts that were with him in the ark. And God made a wind to blow on the earth, to dry up the sea. There was no more rain, and the springs of the deep were dry. And the sea fell from the land each day, so that when six months were gone, the ark had rest on the hills of Ararat. The sea went down all the time till the tenth month, and then the tops of the hills could be seen.

Then Noah went to look out from the roof of the ark, and sent forth a large bird, which went to and fro till the sea was gone from off the earth. He sent forth a dove, too, to see if the sea had gone from the face of the ground. But the dove found no rest for the sole of her foot, and she came back to him to the ark; for there was no dry place on the earth; then he put forth his hand, and took her back to him in the ark.

And in one week more he sent forth the dove once more out of the ark; and she came in to him at night; and lo! in her mouth was a leaf from a tree; and so Noah knew that the sea was gone from the land.

And at the end of the next week, he sent forth the dove once more, but she did not come back to him this time, for she was so glad to get out of the ark and in the sweet trees.

At last the sea was gone from the

RETURN OF THE DOVE TO THE ARK

earth, and Noah took off the roof of the ark, and lo, the ground was dry.

And God spoke to Noah, and said, "Go forth out of the ark, thou and thy wife, and thy sons and thy sons' wives. Bring forth with thee all the beasts that are in the ark, and let them roam on the earth, and fill it once more with life."

And Noah did so. And he built a house of praise to the Lord; and took beasts and fowls, and slew them for a burnt gift to the Lord.

And the Lord said, "I will no more curse the ground for man's sake; though he sins all his life; nor will I smite the earth and cut off all life from it, as I have done. While the earth lasts, seed and fruit, cold and heat, day and night, shall not cease"

And God blest Noah and his sons, and said, "Take the earth and rule all things that move in it. I speak this word to you and to your seed; no more shall all flesh be cut off by a flood; there shall be no more flood to drown the earth. And this is the sign that I give you that my word shall not fail as long as the earth lasts. I do set my bow in the cloud, and it shall be for a sign to me and to all the earth. And it shall come to pass, when I bring a cloud on the earth, that the bow shall be seen in the cloud. And then I will think of my word which I spake; and there shall no more be a flood to cut off all flesh from the earth."

When we see the rain bow, we must think of these words of God.

There is an ark now that will save

us from the sea of fire at the last day, as Noah's ark did him. That ark is Christ; if we are His, we are safe from all harm, and He holds us in His arms as the ark held Noah.

God told Noah's sons and his sons' sons not to live all in one place, but to go and spread in the earth. They did not like this; so they said, "Let us make brick and build a town with a high house in it whose top will reach the sky, and let us all live here."

And the Lord came down to see the town and the high place which the men built. Now they all spoke one tongue. But God, to make them spread on the earth, as He had told them to do, made them to speak strange tongues. Then they left off to build, for one could not tell what his brother said. So those who spoke one tongue went to live in one place, and left those who could not speak like them; thus God made them spread in the earth. The name of the high place they tried to build was the Tower of Babel.

Chapter V.

ABRAHAM, THE FRIEND OF GOD.

A long time from the Flood, there was a good man whose name was Abram. Now the Lord had said to Abram, "Get thee out of thy land, and from thy father's house, to a land that I will show thee. And I will bless thee, and make thy name great, and in thee shall all the homes in the world be blest."

Abram did not know where God would take him, or what He would do with him. But he knew that it was the good God who spoke to him, and that He would take care of him, and show him the way; so he left his home, and went just where God told him to go. He had faith in God, and God had love for him, and blest him all the more for his faith. If he had said I will not leave my home and go with God, he would have lost the sweet home that his dear Lord meant to give him in the end.

But he did not fear to go where God led the way; so he went, as the Lord had said to him. He had no child, but his wife Sarah and Lot, his sister's son, went with him. Abram was seventy-five years old when he left his home to go where God should tell him.

Abram was rich, and he took with him his gold, and his flocks and herds, and his men and maids. It was a long train that went with him on their way through the hills and plains. The land where they were was so dry, that when they came to a well or a brook they would stop and rest in the shade of the palm trees, and eat and drink, and give their flocks drink. At night they would pitch their tents near some well. The tired beasts would kneel down and the men would take the loads from off their backs. Abram and Sarah and Lot would get down and go in their tents, where soft mats would be spread for them to sit on, and their slaves would bring them meat and bread and fruit to eat. It was so warm in that land that they could sleep on their mats in their tents. Then the slaves would make a fire near by, and spread their mats on the ground, and some would watch the flocks all night while the rest slept, so that no wild beast or thief should come and take them. Wild beasts will not come near a fire.

So they went on, and if those they met said to them, "Where do ye go with such a long train?" they would say, "God shows us where to go."

Soon they came to the land of Canaan, and as they went through it they saw that the land was full of men who were strange to them.

There the Lord came to Abram, and said, "To thee and to thy sons will I give this land." So this was to be Abram's land, and though it was strange to him, yet he knew what God had said was true, and that He would give it to him; and there he built a great heap of stones, to mark the place where God spoke to him. He was full of love to God, and gave thanks to Him for so sweet a land.

And he went from thence to a hill near Bethel, and put up his tent, and there he built a house to the Lord, and knelt and gave praise to his name. Then he went on, with his face to the south. The flocks must rest each day at noon, and feed on the grass, and all those who were with him must rest too, and at night they put up their tents and all slept. The mothers and the children rode on the asses, and the fathers went by their side. Abram and Sarah and Lot rode in the midst of their slaves.

But now there had been no rain for a long time; the streams were dry, and the grass dead, and there was no food for them to eat, so they had to leave Canaan for a time, and go down to Egypt, where there is a stream, the Nile. This stream does not dry up, but keeps the ground moist and the grass green all the year round.

They were in Egypt for a while, and then all went back to Canaan. Abram now had more wealth than he had had at a time in all his life. His flocks and herds were so large, and Lot's were so large too, that they had to part. They could not find grass in one place to feed them all, and their slaves would fight for what there was. So Abram said to Lot, "Let there be no strife, I pray thee, with me and thee, and with my slaves and thy slaves, for we are brothers. Is not the whole land ours? If thou wilt take the left hand, then I will go to the right; or if thou go to the right, then I will take the left."

How well it was for them not to fight! Abram had much love for God and for his brother too, so he would give up. He did not say to Lot, "I want this, and you must take that; but he said take what you choose, and I will then take the rest. Can we not be like Abram, and give up to our brother?

Lot saw a rich plain not far off, the plain of Jordan. It was like Egypt, moist and green, for the stream ran through it, and Lot thought he should like much to live there. So he chose all the plain of Jordan, and took his flocks and herds and went his way.

Then Abram dwelt in the land of

Canaan, and Lot dwelt in the towns of the plain, and put up his tents near Sodom. But though Sodom was so fine to look at, the men there were bad, and it made Lot, who was good, feel sad to see them.

When Lot had gone, the Lord said to Abram, "Lift up now thine eyes and look from the place where thou art, north and south and east and west, for all the land which thou dost see I will give to thee and to thy seed. And I will make thy seed as the dust of the earth; so that if a man can count the dust of the earth, then shall he count thy seed. Rise, walk through the land in the length of it and in the breadth of it, for I will give it all to thee."

Then Abram took up his tent and came and dwelt in the plain of Mamre, which is in Hebron, and built there a place of prayer to the Lord. In each place where Abram dwelt, he put up a heap of stones, on which he laid the lambs which he gave to God, and where he knelt and gave thanks to the Lord.

All this time Abram had no child, but God told him that he should have a child, and he was sure that he should when God said so. This was faith. Abram's faith made God love him more. And He spoke to him in a dream, and said, "Fear not, Abram, I am thy shield, and will do thee good."

When Abram was ninety-nine years old, the Lord came to him again, and said to him, "I am the Lord thy God, walk with me, and be good, and I will love thee and bless thee."

And Abram fell on his face, and God spoke with him, and said, " I will be a God to thee, and to thy seed. And I will change thy name to Abraham in place of Abram."

God tells us in His word that He loves us, and will take care of us here, and give us a sweet home on high with Him, and we must love Him and thank Him for it as Abraham did. How wrong it would be to doubt what God says!

One day Abraham sat in his tent door, in the plains of Mamre, in the heat of the day, when lo! three men stood near him. And when he saw them, he ran to meet them from the tent door, and bent low, with his face to the ground.

And he said, " My Lord, if now I

have found grace in thy sight, go not, I pray thee, from me."

"Let my slaves wash your feet, and rest near this tree" (in those days they did not wear shoes like ours, but soles, and straps to tie them on the feet, and as it was hot and there was much dust, when they came to a friend's tent, he would take off the straps, and wash their feet).

So Abraham said, "I pray you, wash your feet, and I will bring some bread; and rest ye your hearts; then you may pass out, but you came to me to rest."

And they said, "Do as thou hast said." Then Abraham went in the tent to Sarah, and said, "Make haste to get some fine meal, knead it, and make cakes on the hearth."

And he ran to the herd, and brought a calf, young and good, and gave it to a young man to dress and cook, so that his friends might eat.

Then he took the cakes and milk, and the calf which he had brought from the herd, and gave it to them; and he stood by them in the shade of the tree, while they did eat.

How kind Abraham was to these strange men. They were sent from God, though he did not know it, but he knew they were in need of food, and he fed them, and gave them rest.

We should be like Abraham in this, and be kind to those that come to our door.

When the men had had food and rest they rose up, and Abraham went with them to bring them on the way.

These men were sent from God to Sodom, to tell Lot to flee out of the town, for God would burn it up the next day, it was such a bad place.

So they went to Sodom and were with Lot all that night; and the next day they took his hand and the hand of his wife and the hands of his two daughters, (for God would not have them hurt,) and led them out of the town, and said to them, "Run for your lives; look not back, nor stay in all the plain; run to the hills, lest ye be burnt."

And Lot said to them, "Oh, not so, my Lord! If I have found grace in thy sight, so that thou wilt save my life, let me flee to this small town near by, for I can not run as far as the hills, lest some harm take me and I die."

And he said to him, "See, I have heard, and will do what you ask, I will not hurt this small town; but haste thee to it, for I can not do my work till thou art gone." The name of the town was Zoar.

The sun rose on the earth as Lot came to Zoar. Then the Lord sent fire on Sodom and on Gomorrah from on high, and burnt up those towns, and all the plain, and all who were there, and that which grew on the ground. Where those great towns once stood, full of men who were so bad, now lies the Dead Sea, a great lake which is so salt, and smells so bad, that no fish can live in it. When we look at the Dead Sea, and think of those towns that were once there, it shows us what God will do to all bad men when he comes to judge the world.

But Lot's wife, though she was told not to look back on to the town, did so, and God made her turn to salt.

The next day Abraham went to look at Sodom and Gomorrah, and at all the land of the plain, and lo, the smoke went up from it as the smoke of a fire.

But when God thus dealt with those bad towns, for Abraham's sake, he brought Lot safe out of the fire, to live up in the hills. He will not let the good be hurt with the bad, but will bring them safe out of harm's way.

CHAPTER VI.

ABRAHAM'S SON.

AT last, when Abraham was an old man, God gave him a son, just as he had faith all this time that God would do as he said, and now he was full of joy and praise. The name he gave his son was Isaac, and he gave him to the Lord from his birth.

And the child grew large and strong, and when he was a year old, Abraham made a great feast, and all his friends came to wish him joy, and to see his son.

Sarah had a slave whose name was

Hagar, and twice she sent her off, and would not let her stay with her. So poor Hagar went out and did not know who would take care of her. But God, who is so kind to all the poor and sad, saw her tears as she sat far off by a spring that sprang up on the dry plain, and said to her "Hagar, Sarah's maid, where didst thou come from, and where wilt thou go?" And she said, "I flee from the face of Sarah."

And the Lord said to her, "Go back and do as Sarah bids thee."

And she said, "Thou God seest me;" for she thought "God saw me all the time, though I did not see him or think of him." How near God is to us, though we may be far off from all men!

The next time that Sarah sent her off, Hagar had her boy Ishmael with her. Sarah told her to go, and not to come back. Abraham, kind and good as he was, did not like to have poor Ishmael sent off; but still he thought it was best, so one day he got up when the sun rose, and took meat and drink, and gave them to Hagar, and sent her off with the child.

So she went up and down in the land of Beersheba, till her food and drink were all gone. Then she put the child down at the foot of a bush, and she went and sat down a good way off, as far as a bow would shoot; for she said, "Let me not see the death of the child." And she sat there and wept.

But the same God who took care of her when she was lost the first time, saw her now, and came to help her. He heard the voice of the lad as he cried, and he spoke to Hagar from on high, and said to her, "What ails thee, Hagar? fear not; for God hath heard the voice of the lad where he is. Rise, lift him up, and hold him with thine hand, for I will bless him and make him great."

Then God told her where to look for a spring, and she found it, and went and gave the lad drink. How her heart beat for joy, as she gave her boy drink and blest God that he need not die of thirst on the hot, dry ground. By the cool well there was a great old tree, and there she laid her boy to sleep, while her full heart gave thanks to God.

When we feel sick or sad or lone, we must think how God took care of Hagar and Ishmael, and how he is near to us when we least think of him.

Now it came to pass when Abraham was old that God did try him, and said to him, "Abraham;" and he said, "Lo, here I am." And he said, "Take now thy son, thy dear son Isaac, whom thou dost love, and go to the land of Moriah, and give him there to me to be slain, just as thou dost slay the lambs and give their blood for thy sins."

Oh, how hard this was for Abraham! Kill his dear son! What did God mean? He did not know, but he knew that God was kind and good, and that he could trust him, and do just what he said. So with a sad heart he rose up at day break, and took his ass to ride, and two of his young men with him, and Isaac his son, and cut the wood to make a fire with, and set out to go to the place of which God had told him.

On the third day, Abraham saw the place far off. And he said to his young men, " Stay here with the ass; and I and the lad will go and pray to God, and come back to you."

And he took the wood and laid it on Isaac his son; and he had the fire in his hand and a knife, and they went on, both of them. Then Isaac spoke to his father, and said, " My father;' and he said, " Here am I, my son."

And he said, " Lo, here are the fire

and the wood, but where is the lamb we shall kill?"

And Abraham said, "My son, God will give us a lamb." So they went on up the hill, the father and the child.

And they came to the place which God had told him of, and Abraham built up a heap of stones, and laid the wood on it, and bound Isaac his son, and laid him on the wood. Then he put forth his hand and took the knife to slay his son.

But the Lord spoke to him from Heaven, and said, "Abraham, Abraham!" and he said, "Here am I."

And He said, "Lay not thine hand on the lad, nor do harm to him; now I know that thou art good, for thou hast not kept back thy son, thy dear son from me."

And Abraham saw a ram near by, caught in the trees by his horns, and he went and took the ram, and slew him for a burnt gift in the place of his son.

And he gave a name to the place where God spoke to him; he called it Jehovah-Jireh—in the mount of the Lord it shall be seen.

And the Lord spoke to Abraham once more, and said, "I have sworn, saith the Lord, since thou hast done this thing, and hast not kept back thy son, thy dear son, from me, that I will bless thee more and more, and I will make thy seed as the stars, and as the sand on the sea shore, and thy seed shall rule all his foes. And in thy seed shall all the earth be blest."

God kept his word to Abraham, for

Christ, who came to bless and save all the world, was the seed or child of Abraham.

So Abraham took his dear son home with joy, and was full of love and faith in God.

Chapter VII.

ISAAC AND REBEKAH.

Now Abraham was old and the Lord had blest him in all things. His great wish was to see his son Isaac have a good wife; so he said to an old man who took care of his house and of all that he had "Thou shalt not take a wife for my son out of this land, but thou shalt go to my old home, and to my kin, and take a wife for my son Isaac." And the man said to him, "What if the maid will not come with me to this land; must I then bring thy son back to the land from which thou didst come?"

And Abraham said to him, "Take care that thou bring not my son back there. The Lord God which took me from my old home, and which spake to me, and said, 'To thy seed will I give this land,' He shall go with thee, and thou shalt take a wife for my son from thence. And if the maid will not come with thee, then thou wilt have done all I have told thee; but bring not my son back there."

And the man told Abraham he would do all he said. So he took all things he would need (for all the goods of Abraham were in his care), and he rose and went to the place where Nabor, Abraham's brother, dwelt.

And as the sun set he came near to the town. And he made his beasts kneel down by a well; he knew they would come out from the town to draw from the well.

And he said, "O Lord God of Abraham, I pray thee send me good speed this day, and show thy love to Abraham. Lo, I stand here by the well; and the maids will come out to fill their jugs; and let it come to pass that the maid to whom I shall say, 'Let down thy jug, I pray thee, that I may drink,' and she shall say, 'Drink, and I will give thy beasts drink, too;' let the same be she that thou hast sent for Isaac; and so shall I know that thou dost show thy love to Abraham."

And it came to pass, while he spoke, that lo, Rebekah, Abraham's niece, came out with her jug in her hand. And the maid was fair to look at; and she went down to the well, and when her jug was full she came up.

And the man ran to meet her,

and said, "Give me, I pray thee, to drink."

And she said, "Drink, my lord," and she made haste, and held the jug to him, and gave him drink. And when he had drunk, she said, "I will draw some for thy beasts too, till they have drunk."

And she made haste, and when the trough was full she ran back to the well to draw more, and drew for him and all that were with him.

And the man saw her and held his peace, to see if the Lord had blest him, and would give this maid to Isaac.

And it came to pass, when they had all drunk, that he took two large gold rings for her ears, and two for her arms, and said, "Whose child art thou? Is there room at thy house for us to lodge in?"

And she said, "I am the child of Bethuel, Nabor's son; and we have both straw and feed, and room to lodge in."

Then the man bent down his head and gave praise to God; and he said, "Blest be the Lord God of Abraham for His love and His truth. I was in the way, and the Lord hath led me to the house of Abraham's brother."

Then the maid ran and told all in her house of these things. And her brother, Laban, ran out to the well to see the man. As he went he saw the ear rings and the rings on his sister's arms, and heard her tell all that the man had said. At last they came to him as he stood still by the well.

And Laban said, "Come in, thou blest of the Lord; why dost thou stand here? for I have room for thee in the house, and for all that are with thee." So the man came to the house; and Laban gave straw and feed to his beasts, and did wash his feet and the men's feet that were with him. And they gave him meat to eat; but he said, "I will not eat till I have told you what I was sent for."

And Laban said, "Speak on." And he said, "I am Abraham's man. The Lord hath blest Abraham much, and he is grown great, and hath flocks, and herds, and gold, and men, and maids, and beasts. And he hath one son, and to him will he give all his wealth. And he said to me, 'Thou shalt not take a wife to my son of the maids of

Canaan, the land in which I dwell, but thou shalt go to my father's house, and to my kin, and take a wife to my son.'

"And now, if ye will be kind and true to Abraham, and send the maid to his son, tell me; and if not, tell me; that I may turn to the right hand or to the left."

Then Laban said, "The thing is from the Lord; we will not speak to thee bad or good. Lo, Rebekah is here; take her and go, and let her be Abraham's son's wife, as the Lord hath said."

And it came to pass, that when Abraham's man heard their words, he bent down to the earth and gave praise to the Lord. And he brought forth gold and fine cloth, and gave to

Rebekah; he gave too to her brother and to her mother fine things.

And they did eat and drink, he and the men that were with him, and all slept there that night; but the next day, he said, "Send me now back to Abraham." And Rebekah's brother and mother said, "Let the maid stay with us a few days, at the least ten; then she shall go."

But he said to them, "Keep me not, since the Lord hath blest my way; send me home to Abraham."

And they said, "We will call the maid, and ask her." And they did so, and said to her, "Wilt thou go with this man?" And she said, "I will go."

So they sent Rebekah and her nurse, with Abraham's man, and his men, and blest her.

ABRAHAM'S SERVANT IN THE HOUSE OF BETHUEL

So the man took Rebekah and her maid and went his way.

And Isaac came from the way of the well Lahai-roi; for he dwelt in the south. And he went out in the field to muse as the sun went down; and lo, a train came near to him.

It was Rebekah and her maids, and when she saw Isaac, she got down from the beast on which she rode; for she had said to the man, "Who is this that walks in the field to meet us?" And he had said, "It is Isaac;" then she took a veil, and put it on her head.

And the man told Isaac all things that he had done. And Isaac brought Rebekah to his mother's tent, to be his wife; and he had great love to her, and felt less sad for his mother's death.

Chapter VIII.

JACOB AND ESAU.

Isaac was two score years old when he took Rebekah to be his wife; and they had two sons, Esau and Jacob. As the boys grew up, Esau's joy was to hunt, and to roam in the fields and woods, but Jacob was a plain man, who was more in his tent, and whose work was to take care of the flocks, and till the ground.

Esau was the first born, and in that land the first born had a right to be blest by his father at his death, and to have most of his goods; but Esau was a wild young man, and did not care for his birth right. One day when he came in faint from the field, he saw some red soup which Jacob had made from herbs, and he said, "Feed me, I pray thee, with that same red soup; for I am faint."

And Jacob said, "If I will give it to thee, wilt thou sell me thy birth right?"

And Esau said, in his hot haste, "Lo, I am so faint, I shall die, and then what good will my birth right do me?"

And Jacob said, "Swear then to give it to me." So Esau sware that he would; and he sold his birth right to Jacob.

Then Jacob gave Esau bread and soup; and he ate and drank and went his way; thus Esau did not care for his birth right, but sold it for a mess of soup. How could he be such a fool as to care more for a small good now, than for great good by-and-by!

At one time when there was no food in the land, and the ground was dry for want of rain, Isaac went to a place not far off, by name Gerar.

And the Lord came to him there and said, "Go not down to Egypt; stay here in this land, and I will be with thee and bless thee, for to thee and to thy seed I will give all this land, and I will keep the word which I spake to Abraham thy father, and in thy seed shall all the homes in the earth be blest. For Abraham had faith in me and kept my laws."

And it came to pass when Isaac was old, and his eyes were dim, so that he could not see, he sent for Esau, his first born, and said to him, " My son!" and he said, " Lo, here am I."

And Isaac said, " I am old, I know not how soon I shall die, and I would bless thee now as my first born, and mine heir. Take, I pray thee, thy bow, and go out to the field, and bring me some deer, and cook for me deer's meat, such as I love, and bring it to me, that I may eat, and bless thee ere I die."

Rebekah heard what Isaac said to Esau his son. Then Esau went to the field to hunt for deer, and to bring it to his father.

And Rebekah went out and said to Jacob her son, " Lo, I heard thy father say to Esau thy brother, bring me deer's meat, that I may eat and bless thee in the sight of the Lord.

ere I die." Now, my son, do as I tell thee; go to the flock, and fetch me from thence two good kids of the goats, and I will cook some good meat for thy father, such as he loves, and thou shalt bring it to him that he may eat, and bless thee in the place of thy brother."

How wrong and false this was to the poor old father, who was blind and could not see his sons. Jacob knew it was wrong, and he said, "But Esau my brother is a rough man, and I am a smooth man. If my father should feel me, he will know that I am not Esau, and do not speak the truth; and he will not bless me, but will curse me."

And his mother said to him, "On me will be thy curse, my son; do as I say, and go fetch me the kids."

So he went and brought them to his mother, and she made nice meat, such as his father was fond of. And she took fine, soft clothes of her son Esau, which she had in the house, and put them on Jacob. And she put the rough skins of the kids on his hands, and on the smooth part of his neck, and gave him the meat and the bread which she had made.

How mean Jacob must have felt, to dress up thus and go and tell a lie to his father, and get his brother's birth right.

He came to his father, and said, "My father." And he said, "Here am I; who art thou, my son?"

And Jacob said, "I am Esau thy first born; I have done as thou didst tell me; rise, I pray thee, and eat of this deer, that thy soul may bless me."

And Isaac said to his son, " How is it that thou hast found the deer so soon, my son?" And he said, " The Lord thy God brought it to me." Oh how bad and false this was!

And Isaac said to Jacob, " Come near I pray thee, that I may feel thee, my son, to see if thou be my true son Esau or not." And Jacob went near to Isaac his father, and he felt him and said, " The voice is Jacob's voice, but the hands are the hands of Esau." And he knew him not, for the skins on his hands made them feel rough, like the hands of his brother Esau ; so he blest him.

And he said, " Art thou my true son Esau?" And Jacob said, " I am."

And the old man said, " Bring the

dish near to me, and I will eat of my son's deer, that my soul may bless thee." And he brought it near to him, and he did eat, and then he brought him the wine, and he drank.

And his father said to him, "Come near now, and kiss me my son."

How could Jacob kiss his father, and still be so false to him? But he did; he came near, and did as he told him, and the blind old man smelt his clothes, and blest him, and said, "See, the smell of my son is as the smell of a field which the Lord hath blest. God shall give thee the dew of Heaven, and the fat of the earth, and much corn and wine. Let men serve thee, and bow down to thee; be lord to thy brothers, and let thy mother's sons bow down to thee; curst be all those that curse thee, and blest be all those that bless thee."

And it came to pass, as soon as Isaac had blest Jacob, when Jacob was scarce gone out from Isaac his father, that Esau came in from his hunt. And he took the nice meat which his father had told him to get, and brought it to him, and said, "Let my father rise and eat of his son's deer, that thy soul may bless me."

And Isaac, his father, said to him, "Who art thou?" And he said, "I am thy son, thy first born, Esau."

But the blind old man shook with fear and dread when he heard this, and said, "Who? where is he that took deer's meat and brought it to me, and I did eat of it while thou wast gone, and I have blest him; yea, and he must be blest."

And when Esau heard the words of his father, he cried out with a great cry, and said, "Bless me, me too, oh, my father!"

And he said, "Thy brother came with lies, and took from thee thy birth right."

And Esau said, "Canst thou not still bless me too?"

And Isaac said, "Lo! I have made him thy lord, and said that all his brothers should bow down to him; and I have made him mine heir. What shall I do now for thee, my son?"

And Esau said to his father, "Canst thou not bless once more, my father? Bless me, me too, oh, my father!" And Esau wept sore.

And his father said to him, "Lo, thou too shalt have the fat of the earth and the dew of heaven. By thy sword shalt thou live, and thou shalt serve thy brother; but it shall come to pass that when thou shall have the strength, thou shalt break his yoke off thy neck."

Chapter IX.

Jacob.

Esau could not bear Jacob, who had got his birth right from him; and he said in his heart, "As soon as my father is dead, then will I slay my brother."

But when these words of his were told to his mother Rebekah, she sent for Jacob, and said to him, "Lo, thy brother Esau means to kill thee. Now do as I say; rise, flee to Laban, my brother, in Haran; and stay with him a few days, till thy brother's wrath turn from thee, and he think no more of that which thou hast done to him;

then will I send and fetch thee home."

Then Rebekah went to Isaac, and said, "Jacob must not take a wife of the maids of this land, as Esau has done. He must go and get a wife."

So Isaac sent for Jacob, and blest him, and said to him, "Thou shalt not take a wife of the maids of Canaan. Rise, go to Padan-aram, to the house of thy mother's father, and take thee a wife from there. And may God bless thee, as he did Abraham, that thou mayst have this land which God gave to Abraham." So Isaac sent Jacob off to Haran.

So Jacob went out from Beersheba on his way to Haran, and when the sun set, he took some stones and laid his head on them, and lay down to sleep.

JACOB'S LADDER

And he had a dream, and lo! he saw stairs set up on the earth, and the top of them rose to heaven; and lo! the sons of God went up and down on the stairs.

And the Lord stood on the top, and said, "I am the Lord God of Abraham thy father, and the God of Isaac; the land on which thou dost lie, to thee will I give it, and to thy seed. And thy seed shall be as the dust of the earth, and they shall spread to the west and to the east, and to the north and to the south; and in thee and thy seed shall all the homes of the earth be blest."

God said the same thing to Jacob that he had said to Abraham and Isaac. He still said He would send a son who would bless all the world, and He kept His word when He sent Jesus Christ.

And God said to Jacob, " Lo, I am with thee and will keep thee in the place where thou shalt go, and will bring thee back to this land; for I will not leave thee till I have done that which I said to thee."

And Jacob woke out of his sleep, and said, " The Lord is in this place, and I knew it not." And he felt fear and said, " How great is this place? this is the house of God, and this is the gate of Heaven."

And he rose up at dawn, and took the stone on which his head had lain, and set it up to mark the place, and put oil on the top of it. And he gave the name of Bethel to that place.

Then Jacob made a vow, and said,

"If God will be with me, and will keep me in this way that I go, and will give me bread to eat and clothes to put on, so that I come back to my home in peace, then shall the Lord be my God; and this stone which I have set for a sign, shall be God's house; and of all that Thou shalt give me, I will give the tenth to Thee."

Jacob had not been as good as Abraham and Isaac, but he came to love God by and by, while he was far from home.

So he went on his way, and came to the land of the east. And he saw a well in the field, and lo, there were three flocks of sheep by it, for out of that well they drank; and a great stone was on the well's mouth. There all the flocks came to drink, and the men took the stone from the well's mouth, and gave them their drink, and then put the stone back in its place.

Jacob said to the men who were with the flocks, "Whence come ye?" And they said, "From Haran." And he said to them, "Do ye know Laban, the son of Nahor?" And they said, "We do." Then he said to them, "Is he well?" And they said, "He is well, and here comes Rachel, his child, with the sheep."

And he said, "It is yet high day, and not time to fold the sheep; give ye them drink, and go and feed them." But they said, "We can not till all the flocks come. Then they will roll the stone from the well's mouth, and we will give the sheep drink."

While he yet spake with them,

Rachel came with her father's sheep; for she kept them. And it came to pass, when Jacob saw Rachel, the child of Laban, his mother's brother, and the sheep of Laban his mother's brother, that Jacob went near, and took the stone from the well's mouth, and gave the sheep drink. And Jacob did kiss Rachel, and he wept, for it made him think of home and his mother to see her.

And he told Rachel that he was the son of Rebekah, and she ran and told her father.

And when Laban heard that Jacob, his sister's son, had come, he ran to meet him, and gave him a kiss, and brought him to his house. And Jacob told him all the news of Isaac and Rebekah. And Laban said to him,

"Thou art my bone and my flesh; stay with me." So he was there with him for a month.

And Laban said to him, "Why shouldst thou serve me for naught? Tell me, what shall thy pay be?"

Now Laban had two daughters, whose names were Leah and Rachel. Leah had weak eyes, but Rachel was very fair. And Jacob felt great love for Rachel, and said, "I will serve thee seven years for Rachel, thy young daughter." And Laban said, "I will give her to thee; stay with me."

So Jacob did work seven years for Rachel; and they were to him like a few days, for the love he had to her.

Then he said to Laban, "Give me my wife, for I have done thy work seven years for her." So Laban sent for his friends, and made a feast, but in place of Rachel he gave Leah to Jacob. But Jacob did not love Leah, and he said to Laban, "What is this that thou hast done? did I not serve thee for Rachel?" And Laban said, "I can not help it. I must give Leah first, for she is the first born. If thou wilt serve me seven years more, I will give Rachel too." So he gave him Rachel, and Jacob was there with him seven more years.

Then Jacob would have gone home, and said to Laban, "Send me now, that I may go to mine own place, my home." But Laban said, "Stay with me, for I know that the Lord doth bless me for thy sake. Tell me what pay thou dost want, and I will give it." So Jacob told Laban if he would give him sheep and goats for his hire he would stay; and he did so six more years.

Chapter X.

JACOB ON HIS WAY HOME.

Jacob had now been with Laban twenty years, but at the end of that time, God spake to him in a dream, and said, "I am the God of Bethel, where thou didst set up the stones for a sign, and where thou didst vow to serve me; now rise, get thee out from this land, and go back to thine own home."

Then Jacob sent for Rachel and Leah to the field where he was with his flock, and said to them, "I see that your father's face is not as kind to me as it was; but the God of my father hath been with me. Ye know that with all my might I have done my work for your father; he hath not done right to me; but God would not let him hurt me, and hath blest me, and made me rich."

Then Rachel and Leah said to him, "All that God hath said to thee, do."

Then Jacob rose up and set his sons and his wives on the beasts which they were to ride, and he took all his flocks, and all his goods which he had got, to go to Isaac his father in the land of Canaan. Laban went to shear his sheep, and Jacob stole off while he was gone, and told him not that he fled; for he thought Laban would still try to make him stay.

And it was told Laban on the third day, that Jacob had fled. And he took his men with him, and went to catch him seven days; at last he came up with him in the mount Gilead. But God came to Laban in a dream that night, and said to him, "Take heed that thou speak not to Jacob, good or bad."

Now Jacob had his tent in the mount, and Laban went there with his men. And Laban said to Jacob, "What hast thou done, that thou hast fled, and did not tell me, that I might have sent thee off with mirth and with songs, with lute and harp; and hast not let me kiss my sons and my daughters? I could do you hurt if I chose, but the God of your father spake to me last night, and said, "See thou speak not to Jacob, good or bad."

And Jacob said, "I thought thou wouldst take by force thy daughters from me. I know thou dost not love me, though I have done well for thee all these years. I have kept thy flock day and night; by day the heat fell on me, and the frost by night, and my sleep went from me. Thus have I been twenty years; and thou hast not been just in my pay. If the God of my fathers, the God of Abraham and the Fear of Isaac, had not been with me, thou wouldst have sent me off poor. But God hath seen my toil, and told thee last night not to hurt me."

And Laban said, "Let us now make a vow that we will be friends, I and thou, and let it be for a sign to us."

And Jacob took a stone, and set it up for a sign ; and they all took stones, and made a heap, and they did eat there on the heap. And Laban said, "This heap is a sign to me and thee this day. The Lord watch me and thee, when thou art gone. This heap shall be a sign, that I will not pass it to harm thee, and thou shalt not pass it to harm me."

Then Jacob did pray, and gave gifts to God, and they did eat bread and were there all night on the mount. And at dawn Laban rose up and gave a kiss to each of his sons and his daughters, and blest them ; and Laban went back to his place.

And Jacob went on his way, and

the sons of God met him. And when Jacob saw them he said, "This is God's host," and he gave a name to that place.

And Jacob sent some of his men to the land of Seir to see Esau his brother; and he told them, "Thus shall ye speak to my lord Esau; Jacob saith thus: I have been with Laban till now; and I have flocks and herds and slaves; and now I am on my way home, and I have sent to tell my lord, that I may find grace in thy sight."

Jacob thought that his brother Esau would hurt him, for he had done so much wrong to Esau in the days gone by.

And the men came back to Jacob and said, "We saw thy brother Esau, and he comes to meet thee, and four hundred men with him."

Then Jacob had much fear, and he set all that he had, the flocks and the herds and all the beasts, in two bands, and said, "If Esau come to the one band and smite it, then the band which is left shall flee."

And Jacob said, "Oh God of my father Abraham, and God of my father Isaac, the Lord which said to me, go back to thy land and to thy home, and I will deal well with thee; I am not worth the least of all the love and of all the truth which thou hast had to me; for with my staff I did cross this Jordan, and now I come back with two bands; save me, I pray thee, from the hand of my brother, from the hand of Esau; for I fear him lest he will come and smite me and the mother with the little ones. But thou didst say, I will do thee good, and make thy seed as the sand of the sea."

And he was there all that night, and took from his flocks a gift for his brother Esau, two hundred she-goats, and twenty he-goats, two hundred ewes, and twenty rams, forty cows and ten bulls.

And he gave them to his men, by droves, and said to them, "Pass the Jordan, but have a space from one drove to the next."

And he said to the man with the first drove, "When Esau my brother meets thee, and says to thee, 'Whose are these, and where dost thou go?' then thou shalt say, 'They are Jacob's; it is a gift sent to my Lord Esau; and lo, he too comes on with us.'"

And so he told all the men that had the droves, "In this way shall ye speak to Esau, when ye find him; and all of you must say, Jacob comes." For he said, "I will soothe him with the gift, and then I will see his face; thus he will not hate me."

Poor Jacob! he knew that he had done so much wrong to Esau, that he must fear to meet him. We too fear those whom we have hurt.

So the gift went through Jordan; and Jacob was that night in his camp, but in the night he rose up, and took his two wives and his eleven sons, and sent them through the ford; he did not go, but went back to pray. He was in prayer all night, as though he must get from God his wish, and at break of day he said to the Lord, "I will not let thee go, till thou bless me." And God said to him, "What is thy name?" And he said, "Jacob."

And God said, "Thy name shall be no more Jacob, but Israel; for as a prince hast thou strength with God and with men, and thou shalt have thy prayer."

And Jacob said the name of that place should be Peniel; for he said, "I have seen God face to face, and yet I live."

Jacob had faith that God would hear his prayer, and so he made it with all his heart, and though he had done so much that was wrong in his youth, God heard his prayer and blest him; for God will hear and bless all who put their trust in him, and will blot out their sins.

The sun rose as Jacob went through Jordan; and lo, Esau came, and with him four hundred men. But Jacob did not fear now, for he knew God would keep him. If we pray and trust like Jacob, we shall not fear what man can do to us.

And Jacob gave his sons to their mothers, and had Leah and her sons go first, and Rachel and her boy Joseph last. And he went in front of them, and bent to the ground seven times till he came near to his brother.

But Esau ran to meet him, and fell on his neck and gave him a kiss, and they wept. And when Esau saw the wives and children, he said, "Who are those with thee?" And he said, "The sons which God gave me."

Then Leah and her sons came near and bent low to the ground, and Joseph too, and Rachel, drew near and bent down.

And Esau said, "What means all this drove which I met?" And Jacob said, "These are to find grace in the eyes of my lord."

And Esau said, "I do not need them, my brother; keep what thou hast for thine own." And Jacob said, "Nay, I pray thee, if now I have found grace in thy sight, then take this gift at my hand, for now I have seen thy face, and thou dost love me. Take it, I pray thee, for God hath blest me, and I have more than I need."

How much Jacob had learnt since

the time when he would cheat his brother, and take from him his birth right! Now he loves him, and wants to do him good.

So Esau took the gift, and said, "Let us go on, and I will go in front of thee." But Jacob said, "My lord knows that my sons are young, and I have young flocks and herds; if they should go too fast, all the flock will die. Let my lord, I pray thee, go on, and I will go as fast as my flocks and my children can, till I come to my lord to Seir."

And Esau said, "Let me then leave some of my men with you, to take care of you." But Jacob said, "What needs it? Let me find grace in the eyes of my lord, and do as I say."

So Esau went back with his troop

to Seir, where they dwelt, and went out to hunt and to roam on the hills and plains, to gain their food by their bows. They must have been glad of the flocks and the herds that Jacob gave them. They were brave men, and could fight well, and take good care of a troop like Jacob's; but Jacob had God to take care of him, and he did not fear. He took some rest at Succoth, and made a house, and booths for his flocks. Then he was at Shechem for a time, and bought a field, and spread his tent there. So he went on.

At Shechem God said to him, "Rise, go up to Bethel, and dwell there." So he came to Bethel, the place where he had had that strange dream, and where God had blest him.

And God spake once more to him there, and said, "The land which I gave Abraham and Isaac, to thee will I give it, and to thy seed." And God went up from him in the place where he spake to him. And Jacob set up a heap of stones in the place, and put a gift of oil on it.

As they went on from Bethel, Rachel died; and Jacob laid her to rest in Bethlehem, and set up a stone to mark her grave; it is there to this day.

At last Jacob came to Isaac his father to Hebron, where Abraham and Isaac had dwelt so long. And Isaac died, old and full of days; and his sons Esau and Jacob laid him in the grave.

Chapter XI.

Joseph.

Joseph was the son of Jacob and Rachel; his mother died at Bethlehem, on her way from her father's nouse to her new home in Canaan; so poor Joseph had no mother. He had ten brothers, who were all grown up when he was a boy, and one young brother, Benjamin. His work was to go out with his brothers, and take care of his father's flocks.

Now Israel had more love for Joseph than for all his grown up sons, for he was the child of his old age, and his mother was dead; and he made him a coat of all hues—red, and blue, and white, and green. And when his brothers saw that their father thought more of him than of them, they would not bear him, or have any peace with him.

One night Joseph had a dream, and the next day he told it to his brothers and they had still less love for him when he had told it. He said to them, " Hear, I pray you, this dream which I have had. For lo, I saw in my dream that we bound up sheaves of grain in the field, and lo, my sheaf rose, and stood up ; and your sheaves stood round, and bent down to my sheaf."

And his brothers said to him, "Shalt thou then rule us?" And they felt more and more hate to him for his dream and for his words.

And he had one more dream, and told it to his brothers, and said, "Lo, I have had a dream more; and lo, the sun and the moon and the eleven stars bent down to me." And he told it to his father, too; but his father chid him, and said to him, "What is this dream that thou hast had? Shall I and thy mother and thy brothers come to bow down to thee to the earth?"

And his brothers felt hate to him, but his father thought on what he said.

One day his brothers went to feed their father's flock in Shechem. And Israel said to Joseph, "Do not thy brothers feed the flock in Shechem? Come, and I will send thee to them." And Joseph said, "Here am I."

And his father said to him, "Go, I pray thee, see if it be well with thy brothers, and well with the flocks; and bring me word." So he sent him out of the vale of Hebron, and he came to Shechem. But he lost his way in the fields; and as he went up and down to look for his brothers, he met a man who said to him, "What dost thou seek?" And he said, "I seek my brothers; tell me, I pray thee, where they feed their flocks."

And the man said, "They are gone from here; for I heard them say, "Let us go to Dothan." So Joseph went to seek them, and found them in Dothan.

And when they saw him far off, while he had not come near to them, they felt such hate to him, that they laid a plot to slay him.

And they said, "Lo, here comes

the one who dreams! Come now, let us slay him, and cast him in some pit; and we will say, some wild beast has torn him; then we will see what will come of his dreams."

But when Reuben, the first born of the ten brothers, heard it, he would not let them do so, but said, "Let us not kill him; shed no blood, but cast him in this pit in the woods, and lay no hand on him." He said this that he might rid him out of their hands, to bring him safe to his father.

And it came to pass, when Joseph was come to his brothers, that they stript off his coat, his coat of all hues, that was on him, and they took him and cast him a pit; the pit was deep and dark, but it was dry. Then with hard hearts, that did not care for their

JOSEPH SOLD BY HIS BRETHREN

brother's tears, they sat down to eat bread ; and as they did so, a troop of Ishmaelites came by from Gilead, with spice and balm and myrrh, on their way to take it down to Egyyt.

And Judah said to his brothers, "What good will it do us if we slay our brother, and hide his blood? Come, let us sell him to the Ishmaelites, and let not our hand be on him ; for he is our brother and our flesh." And they all thought this plan was a good one.

Then the Ishmaelites came by : and the brothers drew Joseph out of the pit, and sold him to them. Poor lad! how he did weep, and pray them not to sell him for a slave! But they would not hear. So the Ishmaelites took him and went on their way to Egypt.

What bad men those brothers were; they would kill poor Joseph or sell him for a slave, so that their father need not love him more than them. They thought he would be first in their father's eyes, and so they put him out of the way. Oh, how wrong it is to want to be first, and to hate our brothers or sisters when we think they have more love than we!

When Reuben came back to the pit and saw that Joseph was not there, he rent his clothes for grief. And he came to his brothers and said, "The child is not; and I, where shall I go?"

Then they took Joseph's coat, and they slew a kid of the goats, and put the coat in the blood. And they brought the coat of all hues to their father, and said, "This have we found;

know now if it be thy son's coat or not."

And he knew it, and said, "It is my son's coat; a wild beast hath caught him; Joseph is no doubt dead." And Jacob rent his clothes and wept for his son a long time.

And all his sons and all his daughters rose up to soothe him; but he would not heed them; for he said, "I will mourn for my son till I go down to the grave." Thus his father wept for him.

If those bad men had any hearts, how they must have felt to see their father weep for his lost child, when they had sold him for a slave. Their sin came back to curse them each day when their father wept, and would not see them, or love them.

When the Ishmaelites got to Egypt, they sold Joseph to Potiphar, a great and rich man.

Did Joseph weep and mourn and waste his life in Egypt, when he was sold for a slave and had to leave his own fair home? No; he knew that God was with him, and that he must be a good man, and do all the good he could in the world. And the Lord blest him while he was in the house of the Egyptian.

His lord Potiphar saw that God was with him, and blest all that he did. So Joseph found grace in Potiphar's sight, and he made him rule his house, and all that he had he put in his hands. And it came to pass, that from the time that he had made him rule, God blest the house for Joseph's sake; He blest all in the house and all in the field. For God has said he will bless the house where the good live

So Joseph would have been well off; but Potiphar's wife did not like him, and told bad lies of him, so that Potiphar was wroth with him, and put him in the jail, a place where the king of Egypt put all who had done wrong. Joseph was thrown in the jail; but the Lord was with him, and gave him grace in the sight of the man who kept the jail, so that he gave up to Joseph's care all those who were there, and he took care of all that was done. Joseph took such good care of all things, that the head man in the jail gave up to him more and more; for the Lord was with him, and blest all that he did.

So Joseph had joy and peace, and did good to all round him, though he was in a jail. He put his love and trust in God, and God was with him and blest him.

Now it came to pass that Pharaoh, the king of Egypt, was wroth with two of his chief men, the chief of those who had the care of his wine, and the chief of those who made bread for him. And he put them in the jail where Joseph was bound.

The head of the guard gave Joseph the care of these men, and he was with them all the long time that they were in the jail. One night these men both had a dream, each man his dream in the same night.

And when it was day, and Joseph came in to see them, lo, they were sad.

And he said to them, "Why look ye so sad to-day?"

And they said to him, "We have had a dream, and there is no one to tell us what it means." And Joseph said to them "God can show us what it means; tell me it, I pray you."

So the man who had the care of the wine told his dream first to Joseph, and said to him, "In my dream, lo, I saw a vine; and on the vine were three boughs; and they brought forth first buds, then bloom, and then ripe grapes. And Pharaoh's cup was in my hand; and I took the grapes and made wine in Pharaoh's cup, and I gave the cup to Pharaoh."

And Joseph said to him, "This is what it means; the three boughs are three days. In three days shall Pharoah lift up thine head, and bring thee back to thy place ; and thou shalt hand Pharaoh's cup to him, in the same way as when thou wast in his house. But think on me when it shall be well with thee, and be kind, I pray thee, to me, and speak of me to Pharaoh, and bring me out of this house. For they stole me out of the land of the Hebrews, and here too have I done no wrong, that they should put me in jail."

When Pharaoh's chief cook saw that the dream was good, he said to Joseph, "I too had a dream, and lo, I had three white plates on my head, and in the top plate there were all kinds of meats for Pharaoh, and the birds did eat them out of the dish on my head."

And Joseph said, "The dream means this; the three plates are three days. In three days shall Pharaoh lift up thy head from off thee, and shall hang thee on a tree, and the birds shall eat thy flesh from off thee."

And it came to pass on the third day, which was Pharaoh's birth day, that he made a great feast; and he took out of the jail both these men. And the first gave the cup to him as he did of old; but the chief cook was hung, as Joseph had said to them.

Yet the man who was brought back to his place did not think of Joseph at all. So poor Joseph was still in the jail; but the Lord thought of him, and made a way to bring him out at last.

Chapter XII.

PHARAOH'S DREAM.

At the end of two full years from this time Pharaoh, the King of Egypt, had a dream: he stood by the Nile; and lo, there came up out of its stream seven fair, fat cows; and they fed in a field. And lo, seven more cows came up out of the stream, poor and lean; and they stood by the fat cows on the brink of the stream. And the poor lean cows did eat up the seven fair, fat cows. So Pharaoh woke.

And he slept, and dreamt once more: he saw in his dream seven ears of corn come up on one stalk, rank and good, and seven thin ears, spoilt with the east wind, spring up by their side. And lo, the seven thin ears ate up the seven rank and full ears. And Pharaoh woke, and lo, it was a dream.

In those days God spoke to men in dreams, and told them what He would do to them and to the world.

So Pharaoh knew his strange dream must mean some strange thing, and the next day his head was full of it, and he felt he must know what it meant; so he sent for all the wise men of Egypt, and told them his dream; but there were none of them that could tell at all what it meant. The lean cows to eat up the fat ones, and the thin ears of corn the good ones! What could it mean?

But when they could find no word

that would please and suit the king, all at once the chief man who had the care of Pharaoh's wine, the one who had been in the jail, thought of Joseph, and of all he had done for him, and he spake to Pharaoh, and said, "I do think on my faults this day; Pharaoh was wroth with me, and put me in ward in the guard's house, both me and the chief cook; and we had a dream in one night, I and he; we had each of us a dream that meant a strange thing.

"And there was in the jail with us a young man, a Jew, slave to the head of the guard, and when we told him our dreams, he told us what they meant; and it came to pass as he told us, so it was; Pharaoh brought me back to my place, but the cook was hung."

Then Pharoah sent for Joseph, poor Joseph, who had been in the jail so long that no one thought of him any more, and it was as though he would have to stay there all his life. But Joseph had been good and brave, and had done his best to serve God in the jail, and God would not leave him to die there, but would bring him out in His own time and way. Some times it may seem as though God did not think of us, but left us to a hard, sad life. But it is not so; God makes His plans in the best way, and comes to us when He sees it is right for us to come out of our grief. And if Joseph could trust God in a dark cell, and love Him still, can we not bear our small pains, and trust Him too?

They brought Joseph in haste out

of his cell, for the king had sent for him, and what kings say must be done quick. And oh, how glad was Joseph to see the light of day, and to breathe the fresh air once more! In a very short time he came in to the king.

Then Pharaoh said to Joseph, "I have had a dream, and there is none that can tell me what it means; and I have heard say of thee that thou canst tell all dreams."

And Joseph said to Pharoah, "It is not in me to know, but God shall give Pharaoh a word of peace."

Joseph was not proud, but gave all the praise to God, who had made him to know His word.

Then Pharaoh told all his dream to Joseph, and said, "I have told this to my wise men, and they could not tell me at all what it meant."

Joseph said to Pharaoh, "The two dreams of Pharaoh are one: they both mean the same thing; God hath told Pharaoh what He will do. The seven good cows are seven years, and the seven good ears of corn are seven years. And the seven thin cows that came up last out of the stream are seven years; and the seven thin ears of corn hurt by the east wind, are seven years of want. This is the thing which I just said to Pharaoh; what God is to do He shows to the king.

"Lo, there shall come seven years of great crops through all the land of Egypt; and at the end of those years shall come seven years of great want;

there shall be no food in the land; it shall bring forth no grain. Then the want of food will be so great that the seven good years will seem as though they had not been. And since the dream came twice, it shows that the thing is sure, and God will soon bring it to pass.

"Now let Pharaoh look out a man good and wise, and have him look to the land of Egypt; and let him chose men to take care of the land, and take up the fifth part of the crops in the seven good years.

"So let them get all the food of those good years that will come first, and lay it up where Pharaoh can take care of it, and keep it in all the towns. And that food shall be for a store to the land when the seven years of want come, so that man and beast need not die of want."

And the thing was good in the eyes of Pharaoh and all his court. And Pharaoh said, "Can we find such a man as this is, a man to whom God tells all that He will do?"

Then Pharaoh said to Joseph, "God hath told thee all this, and there is none so wise as thou art. Thou shalt be that great man who shall rule all Egypt as thou hast said. Thou shalt be as great as I am, save the throne. See! I have set thee to rule all the land of Egypt."

And he took off his ring from his hand and put it on Joseph's hand, and put fine clothes on him, and a gold chain round his neck.

And he made him to ride with the

king, and all said, "Bow the knee!" So they knelt to Joseph, and he had rule in the land, next to the king.

Thus God took Joseph out of a dark, damp cell, and set him next to the throne. So He puts men down and takes them up, just as He will. Joseph had not lost his faith in God in the jail, now let us see if he lost it in the king's court.

Pharaoh thought a great deal of Joseph, so much that he said, "I am Pharaoh, and I say that no man shall lift hand or foot in all the land of Egypt but with thy leave."

And he gave him a new Egyptian name, and gave him for his wife the child of one of the priests of Egypt. So Joseph went out through all the land of Egypt, and God made him so wise that he could take care of that great land, though he was but thirty years old, and had been brought up in the fields to take care of flocks. But he was so just that all men had faith in him.

Then came the seven good years, and the earth brought forth much grain. And Joseph took some of the food of those seven years, and laid it up in the towns; in each town he laid up the corn that grew in the fields round it. So he got corn as the sand of the sea; so much that at last he could not count it.

As the men of the land saw Joseph while he did this, they must have thought it so strange that he should know just what would come, and how to lay up for the time to come. The land was full of food, the sky was blue and calm, the fields were green, and the blue Nile ran to the sea. It did not look as though there would be sore want in so short a time; and some, no doubt, would say, "How knows this man more than we do? There will be no seven years of want; we will not lay up our grain. He says his God tells him, but we do not know his God; we have our own gods, our bulls, and calves, and snakes, that are our gods, and they do not tell us this thing—we will not do as he says." But then the king's word would come, and they would have to mind it. For Pharaoh was sure what Joseph said was true, and must have thought in his heart that Joseph's God was the true God. So Joseph, by his deeds, showed his faith in his God, and made the whole land think of Him and fear Him, too.

At last the seven good years came to an end, and now all watch to see if Joseph's words would come true. The barns were full of wheat; the towns had much corn laid up where there would be need of it. Yes! the rains up in the hills did not come; the Nile did not rise up from its banks to flow on the land and make it rich and green, but ran more and more low and small, while the plain grew hard and dry for want of the stream that should come up and wet it each spring. For you must know it does not rain in Egypt. It rains off up in the hills, and fills up the Nile, and that wets the whole land, and makes it bring forth grain when it is sown.

So there was great dearth in Egypt, and the whole land knew that God—Joseph's God—was right, and their false gods were wrong. Now was Joseph's time to do good; the land was full of corn which he had laid up; now he could feed the poor men who would have felt sore want of it had it not been for that. And then, too, the dearth spread to all lands—the crops were poor, and there was no bread; and when they heard how corn had been laid up in Egypt, they all came there to buy of Joseph; for the dearth was so sore in all lands.

Now Pharaoh thought more and more of Joseph and Joseph's God, and when all the land of Egypt had no food and cried to Pharaoh for bread, he said to all the Egyptians,

"Go to Joseph; do what he says." So they came to Joseph from Egypt and from all lands, and his fame was great. The poor young Jew who had put his trust in God through good and bad, who had not lost faith and hope when he was torn from his home and sold to be a slave by his own brothers, who had put up his prayer and praise to God in the jail, and done right in the king's house, was now as great a a prince as there was in all the earth.

CHAPTER XIII.

JOSEPH'S BROTHERS.

THE want of food spread through the land of Canaan, Joseph's old home, where Jacob his father lived. And when Jacob heard that there was corn in Egypt, he said to his ten sons, "Why do ye stand still, while we die of want? Lo, I have heard that there is corn in Egypt; get you down there, and buy for us from thence, that we may live and not die."

So Joseph's ten brothers went down to buy corn in Egypt. But Benjamin, their young brother, who was but a lad, Jacob sent not; for he said, "What if harm should come to him, as it did to Joseph, when that wild beast caught him." Poor man! he did not think that his sons could have told him a lie, and that Joseph was not dead. If he had been told that Joseph was that great man who sold the corn in Egypt, he would not have thought it could be so.

So the sons of Jacob came to buy corn with the rest of the crowd; and they came to Joseph, for he it was that sold to all in the land. And his brothers bent down their heads to the earth; for was he not the great Egyptian prince? So Joseph's old dream came true, that they should all bow down to him.

As soon as Joseph saw his brothers he knew them; but he was not at all like the youth who took care of sheep with them in Canaan; he was a great prince, with his robes and his gold chains and his slaves, and they did not know him at all.

He did not let them know that he knew them, but made as though he was strange to them, and spoke in a rough voice to them, and he said, "Whence come ye?"

And they said, "From the land of Canaan to buy food."

Then Joseph thought of the dreams which he had had of them, how they should bow down to him: and he said to them, "Ye are spies; to see the dearth in this land ye are come."

And they said, "Nay, my lord, but to buy food are we come. We are all one man's sons; we are true men, we are no spies."

And he said to them, "Nay, but tc see the dearth in the land ye are come."

Then they felt great fear of this prince who was so rough to them, and they said, "We are twelve brothers, the sons of one man in the land of Canaan; one, a young lad, is this day with our father; and one is not."

And Joseph said to them, "No, it is as I said, ye are spies. If ye are not, prove it in this way: ye shall not go forth from here, till ye have brought your young brother with you. Send one of you, and let him fetch your brother, and ye shall be kept in jail, that I may know if ye speak the truth or not; or else, by the life of Pharaoh, ye are spies."

And he put them all in jail for three days. And on the third day he said to them, "This do, and live; for I fear God; if ye be true men, let one of you be bound and stay in the jail; and go ye and take corn for your home. But bring the young lad, your brother, to me; so shall I know that your words are true, and ye shall not die." And they said they would do so.

But in much fear and dread they said in their own tongue, (for they thought Joseph was an Egyptian, and would not know what they said,) "Oh! now we feel our sin that we did to our brother Joseph, when we sold him for a slave, and sent him far off from his home. How he did beg and pray us in the grief of his soul, and we would not hear. This thing is come on us for that sin of ours."

And Reuben said to them, "Did I not tell you not to harm the child? and ye would not hear. Lo, now God will do to us as we did to him."

They knew not that Joseph heard them, or that he could speak their tongue. But he went from them and wept, as he heard their talk. Then he came back and spoke to them, and took from them Simeon, and bound him in their sight.

Joseph might now have slain all his brothers, or thrown them in jail, to pay them for what they had done to him. But he did not want to harm them. He did not hate them for their sin; he felt love for them, and a wish to meet them as brothers. But he thought it was not best quite yet to make known to them who he was.

So he told his men to fill their sacks with corn, and to put the gold which they had paid for the corn back in their sacks, and to give them food for the way. Thus he did to them; and they put their sacks on the backs of their beasts and went their way.

But as one of them went to his sack to give his ass corn at the inn, he saw his gold; for lo, it was in the sack's mouth.

And he said to his brothers; "My gold is put back; and lo, it is in my sack." And their hearts were full of fear, and they said, "What is this that God hath done to us?"

And they came to Jacob their father in the land of Canaan, and told him all that had come to them, and said, "The man, who is the lord of the land, was rough to us, and took us for spies. And we said to him, we are true men, we are no spies. We are twelve brothers, sons of our father; one is not, and one, a youth, is this day with our father in the land of Canaan.

"And the man, the lord of the land, said to us, 'In this way shall I know that ye are true men; leave one of your brothers here with me, and take food for your home and be gone; and bring your young brother to me; then shall I know that ye are no spies, but are true men; so will I free your brother, and ye shall trade in the land.'"

And it came to pass as they took

the corn out of their sacks, lo, each man's gold was in his sack; and when both they and their father saw the gold they had fear.

And Jacob their father said to them, "Ye have torn my sons from me; Joseph is not, and Simeon is not, and ye will take Benjamin too: all these things are hard for me."

And Reuben said to his father, "Slay my two sons, if I bring him not back to thee; give him to my care, and I will bring him back safe."

But Jacob said, "My son shall not go down with you; for his brother is dead, and he is all that is left to me of his mother Rachel. If harm should come to him in the way in which ye go, then should ye bring down my grey hairs with grief to the grave."

Still there was great dearth; no food in all the land of Canaan. And it came to pass, when the food was all gone which they had brought out of Egypt, that Jacob said to his sons, "Go, buy us some more corn."

And Judah spake to him, and said, "The man did vow to us, 'Ye shall not see my face, if your young brother be not with you.' If thou wilt send Benjamin with us, we will go down and buy thee food. But if thou wilt not send him, we will not go down; for the man said to us, 'Ye shall not see my face, if your brother be not with you.'"

And Israel said, "Why did ye deal so ill with me as to tell him ye had a brother at home?"

And they said, "The man said so

much to us of our home and of our kin, that we could not help it. He said, 'Does your father still live? Have you a brother at home?' And we told him. How could we know that he would say, 'Bring your brother down?'"

And Judah said to Israel his father, "Send the lad with me and we will rise and go, that we may live and not die, both we, and thou, and our children. I will be sure to bring him back; of my hand shalt thou ask him; if I bring him not to thee, then let me bear the blame for all time. For if it had not been for this, we might have gone and come back with food by this time."

And their father said to them, "If it must be so, now do this: take of the best fruits in the land, and take the man a gift—balm and myrrh, and spice and nuts. And take twice the gold you did to pay for the corn; and the gold that was brought back in the mouth of your sacks, take it back in your hand; it may have been left in there by chance. Take your brother, and rise; go to the man. And God give you grace in the sight of the man, that he may send back Simeon and Benjamin; for if I lose my sons I have lost all."

Chapter XIV.

BENJAMIN.

As soon as their father said that Benjamin might go with them, the men took the gift, and twice the gold, and the lad, and rose up and went down to Egypt; while poor old Jacob, left at home, was full of fear for his boy, and of grief for him and for his lost Joseph. He did not know that God, who had led him all his life, would soon take from him his grief and give him great joy.

So the brothers came to Egypt to Joseph. And when Joseph saw Benjamin with them, he said to the man who took care of his house, "Bring these men in, and have all things done for them; for these men shall dine with me at noon."

And the man did as Joseph bade him, and brought the men to his house. And they had fear when they were brought to his house; and they said, "It must be for the gold that was put back in our sacks, that we are brought in; he seeks to find some fault with us, that he may fall on us, and take us for slaves."

And they came near to Joseph's head man, and spoke with him at the door of the house, and said, "Oh, sir! we did come down the first time to buy food. And it came to pass, when we came to the inn, we went to our sacks, and lo, each man's gold was in the mouth of his sack; and we have brought it back in our hand. And we have brought more gold in our hands to buy food; we do not know who put our gold in our sacks."

And he said, "Peace be to you; fear not; your God and the God of your father, gave you the gold in your sacks; I had it, and put it there." And he brought Simeon out to them.

Then he brought them in, and made them wash their feet; and gave food to their beasts. And they got out their gift for Joseph, when he should come in at noon; for they heard that they should eat bread there.

And when Joseph came home they brought him the gift which was in their hand, and bent down to him to the earth. And he was kind to them, and said, "Is your father well, the old man of whom ye spake? Does he still live?"

And they said, "Our father is in good health; he still lives." And they bent down their heads once more to Joseph.

Thus Joseph's dream came true that his brothers should all bow down to him. It was just that they, who had been so bad, should be made to serve him, the good man. Could they but have known that this lord of Egypt was their own brother Joseph, whom they had put out of their way when he was a child!

Then Joseph cast his eyes long on his brother Benjamin, and said, "Is this your young brother of whom ye spake to me?" And he said, "God bless thee, my son!"

Then he made haste to turn from them; for his heart did yearn for his own brother, the son of his mother Rachel; and he sought where to weep; and he went to his room and wept there. His love and joy were so great to see his own kin once more, he who had been cut off from them all his life.

Then he did wash his face and went out, and put back his tears, and said, "Set on bread." And they set on bread for him, and bread for them, and bread for the Egyptians which did eat with him; for the Egyptians could not eat with the Hebrews, they thought it a sin.

So they sat down, each one in his right place, the first born in the first seat, and Benjamin in the last. And they could not think how Joseph knew the age of each one so as to give each his place.

And he sent meat to them from his own dish; but Benjamin's meat was five times as much as the rest. And they ate and drank, and were glad with him.

And Joseph said to his head man, "Fill the men's sacks with food, as much as they will hold, and put each man's gold in his sack's mouth. And put my cup, from which I drink, in the sack's mouth of the youth, with his gold." And he did as Joseph told him.

As soon as it was light the men were sent off, they and their beasts. And when they were gone out of the town, and not yet far off, Joseph said to his man, "Up! go on to the men;

and when thou dost reach them, say to them, 'Why have ye done harm for good? Is not this my lord's cup in which he drinks? you have done wrong to take it.'"

And he went to them, and spake these same words. And they said, "Why doth my lord say this? God knows that we would not do such a thing. Lo, the gold which we found in our sacks' mouths we brought back to thee out of the land of Canaan; how, then, should we steal out of thy lord's house? If it be found with one of us, let that one die, and we will all be my lord's slaves."

And he said, "Let it be so; he with whom it is found shall be my slave; the rest of you shall be free."

Then each man took down his sack

to the ground to look in it; and the man made a search from the first to the last, and the cup was found in Benjamin's sack.

Then they rent their clothes for grief, put their sacks back on their beasts, and went back to the town.

And Judah and all the brothers came to Joseph's house, for he was yet there, and they fell down to the ground.

And Joseph said, "What deed is this that ye have done? Do ye not know that I have the gift to know all that is done?"

And Judah said, "What shall we say to my lord; how shall we make thee know that we have not done this thing? We did a great sin in the old time, and God hath found us out Lo, we are my lord's slaves, both we and he with whom the cup is found."

And he said, " Nay, it shall not be so; but the man in whose hand the cup is found, he shall be my slave, and as for you, get ye up in peace to your father."

Then Judah came near to him, and said, " Oh, my lord! let me, I pray thee, speak a word in my lord's ear, and be not wroth with me; for thou art as great as Pharaoh. My lord said to us, ' Have ye a father or a brother?' and we said to my lord ' We have a father, an old man, and a child of his old age, a lad, and his brother is dead, and he is all that is left of his mother, and his father loves him. And thou saidst to us, ' Bring him down to me, that I may set my eyes on him.' And we said to my lord, 'The lad can not leave his father, for if he should leave his father his father would die.'

"And thou saidst to us, 'If your young brother come not down with you, ye shall see my face no more.'

"And it came to pass, when we came up to our father, we told him the words of my lord.

"And our father said, 'Go once more and buy us some food.' And we said, 'We can not go down; if our young brother be with us, then we will go down; for we may not see the man's face if he be not with us.' Then my father said to us, 'Ye know that I had two dear sons of my lost wife Rachel; and the one went out from me, and ye know he was torn by a wild beast, and I saw him not since;

and if ye take this, too, from me, and harm come to him, ye shall bring down my grey hairs with grief to the grave.'

"Now when I come to my father, and the lad be not with us, since his life is bound up in the lad's life, it shall come to pass, that when he sees that the lad is not with us, he will die, and we shall bring down the grey hairs of our father with grief to the grave.

"For I made a pledge for the lad to my father, and said, 'If I bring him not to thee, then I shall bear the blame with my father for all time.' Now, I pray thee, let me stay as a slave to my lord, and not the lad; and let the lad go up with his brothers. For how shall I go up to my father and the lad be not with me, lest I see the harm that shall come to my father?"

These brothers, whose hearts were so cold and hard when they sold Joseph, that they did not care for their father's grief, how much more love they had now! They had seen their father's tears, and the cloud which they had brought on the old man, till their hearts had come to melt, and they had felt sharp pangs for their great sin; and now that they were brought to this pass, and knew not which way to turn, they were sore hurt at the thought of their father's woe, when he should find he had lost this child, too. Thus it was that God led them at last to feel their sin.

Joseph could not bear it any more, or keep back his tears, and he cried out, "Let all men go out from me." And there stood no man with him, while Joseph made known to his brothers who he was. And he wept loud, so that the Egyptians and the house of Pharaoh heard him.

And he said to his brothers, "I am Joseph! Doth my father yet live?" And his brothers could not speak to him, for they had great fear of him to whom they had done such a wrong.

And Joseph said to his brothers, "Come near to me, I pray you." Then they came near to him. And he said, "I am Joseph, your brother, whom ye sold to Egypt; now, then, be not sad that ye sold me here, for God did send me to do good and to save life. For these two years hath the dearth been in the land, and there are yet five years in which there shall be no crops to sow or to reap.

" And God sent me here to keep you on the earth, and to save your lives. So now it was not you that sent me, but God."

Good Joseph, full of love, with no hate in his heart to his brothers who had sought to kill him. He did not wish to blame them, but did all he could to soothe them.

And he said, " God hath made me a father to Pharaoh, and lord of all his house, and a prince through all the land of Egypt. Haste ye, and go up to my father and say to him, thus saith thy son Joseph, ' God hath made me lord of all Egypt; come down to me, wait not. And thou shalt dwell in the land of Goshen, and thou shalt be near to me, thou and thy sons, and thy sons' sons, and thy flocks and thy herds, and all that thou hast. And there will I feed thee; for there are yet five years of dearth, lest thou and thy house and all that thou hast, come to want.'

"And lo, your eyes see, and the eyes of my brother Benjamin, that it is my mouth that speaks to you. And ye shall tell my father of all my rank and wealth in Egypt, and of all that ye have seen. And ye shall haste and bring down my father here."

And he fell on his brother Benjamin's neck, and wept; and Benjamin wept on his neck.

And he did kiss all his brothers, and wept with them; and then his brothers spoke long with him.

CHAPTER XV.

JACOB GOES DOWN TO EGYPT.

Now, it was told in Pharaoh's house, "Joseph's brothers are come;" and it made Pharaoh glad, and all his court.

And Pharaoh said to Joseph, "Say to thy brothers, this do ye; lade your beasts, and go, get you to the land of Canaan. And take your father, and all you have, and come to me; and I will give you the good of the land of Egypt, and ye shall eat the fat of the land. Now take you carts out of the land of Egypt for your children and for your wives, and bring your father, and come. Care not for your stuff;

for the good of the land of Egypt is yours."

And the sons of Israel did so; and Joseph gave them carts, as Pharaoh had said, and gave them food for the way. To all of them he gave each man a change of clothes, but to Benjamin he gave five times as much as to the rest.

And to his father he sent ten beasts with the good things of Egypt, and ten more with corn and bread and meat for his father by the way.

So he sent his brothers on their way, and said to them, "See that ye fall not out by the way."

And they went up out of Egypt, and came to the land of Canaan to Jacob their father. And they said to him, "Joseph lives, and he is prince of all the land of Egypt." And Jacob's heart felt faint, for he could not think it was true.

And they told him all the words of Joseph; and when he saw the carts which Joseph had sent to take him, his heart was strong once more, and he said; "It is true; Joseph my son yet lives; I will go and see him ere I die."

So Israel set out to go to Egypt with all that he had; and he came to Beer-sheba, and there he gave gifts and made prayers to the God of his father Isaac. And God spake to him in a dream, and said, "Jacob, Jacob." And he said, "Here am I."

And He said, "I am God, the God of thy father; fear not to go down to Egypt; for I will there make of thee a great race. I will go with thee; and I will bring thee back; and Joseph shall be with thee in thy last days."

And Jacob rose up from Beer-sheba, and his sons took him, and their wives and their children, in the carts which Pharaoh had sent. More than seventy souls there were, and they all came to the land of Egypt.

And Joseph went up to meet Israel his father, to Goshen; and when he saw him, he fell on his neck, and wept there a good while. And Israel said to Joseph, "Now let me die, since I have seen thy face, and thou dost yet live."

And Joseph said to his brothers, "I will go up and tell Pharaoh, 'My brothers, and my father's house, which were in the land of Canaan, are come to me; and the men have sheep, for their trade hath been to feed flocks; and they have brought their flocks and their herds with them.

"And when Pharaoh shall call you, and shall say, 'What is your trade?' ye shall say, 'We have kept flocks from our youth till now, both we and our fathers'; then ye shall dwell in the land of Goshen, for the Egyptians do not like those that keep sheep."

And Pharaoh said to Joseph, "Thy father and thy brothers are come. The land of Egypt is in thy hands; in the best of the land make them dwell, in the land of Goshen."

And Joseph brought in Jacob his father to see Pharaoh, and Jacob blest the king.

And Pharaoh said to him, "How

old art thou?" And Jacob said, "The days of the years of my life are one hundred and thirty years; few and sad have the years of my life been, and my life has not been as long as the life of my fathers." And Jacob blest the king, and went out.

If Jacob had done right when he was young, he would not have said his life had been so sad. But he went wrong first, and though God was so good to him, and blest him in spite of his faults, yet he could not look back with joy on his youth. We must serve God when we are young, if we want to have peace and joy when we grow old.

So Jacob and his sons had a home in Goshen, the best of the land, and Joseph fed them all through the seven years of dearth.

In seventeen years more, Jacob's time came to die; and he called his son Joseph, and said to him, "Lay me not, I pray thee, in Egypt; I would lie with my fathers, and thou shalt take me out of Egypt, and lay me in their tomb." And Joseph said, "I will do so."

And Jacob said to Joseph, "God came to me in the land of Canaan, and blest me, and said, 'I will give this land to thee and to thy seed for all time'."

Then Jacob saw Joseph's two sons, whom he had brought with him, and he said, "Who are these?" For his eyes were dim, so that he could not see well. And Joseph said, "They are my sons."

And Jacob said, "Bring them, I

pray thee, to me, and I will bless them." And he brought them near to him, and he did kiss and bless them, and said, "Joseph, I had not thought to see thy face, and lo, God hath made me see thy sons!" And he blest the lads, and said, "God, with whom my fathers Abraham and Isaac did walk, the God who has fed me all my life long to this day, and hath kept me from all harm, bless the lads, and make them great and good!"

Then Jacob sent for all his sons, and said, "Come to me, that I may tell you that which shall come to you in the last days. All ye sons of Jacob, come here and hear me."

Then he told them what should be to each one when they got back to the land of Canaan. And he said to them, " I die; lay me with my fathers in the cave of Machpelah, in the land of Canaan. There lie Abraham and Sarah his wife; there Isaac and Rebekah, his wife, and there is Leah, my wife."

And when Jacob had told all to his sons, he lay down in his bed and died.

And Joseph fell on his father's face, and did kiss him; and he did mourn for him three score and ten days. When those days were past, he said to Pharaoh, " Let me go up, I pray thee, and lay my father in the tomb of his fathers, and I will come back to thee." And Pharaoh said, " Go."

So Joseph went up, and his brothers, and a long train of Egyptians went with him. And when they had laid Jacob in the tomb, they came back to Egypt.

And Joseph's brothers thought, now that their father was dead, that Joseph would hate them, and pay them back for all the wrong which they had done to him. And they sent word to Joseph, and said, "Thy father told us ere he died, thus shall ye say to Joseph: 'Think not, I pray thee, of the sin of thy brothers; for they did great wrong to thee; but now, I beg thee, think not of it, for the sake of the God of thy father.'"

And Joseph wept when they said this to him. And his brothers went and fell down at his feet, and said, "Lo, we are thy slaves."

And Joseph said to them, "Fear not, for am I in the place of God?

Your sin was to God; kneel to Him. As for you, ye thought to do harm to me, but God meant it for good, as it is this day, to save this land in the time of want. So now fear ye not; I will feed you and your children." And he did cheer them, and was most kind to them.

Joseph's life was a hundred and ten years long; and when he came to die, he said to his brothers, " I die; but God will be sure to come to you, and bring you out of this land to the land which he sware to Abraham, to Isaac and to Jacob." And Joseph made them swear to him that when God came to take them home to Canaan, they would take his bones with them from Egypt home to the land of his fathers.

So Joseph died in full faith in God.

and left us his good life to read, that we may try to be like him. If all boys were like Joseph, how brave they would be to bear pain, as Joseph was in the pit, on the road to Egypt, and in the jail; how they would love those that hate them, and bless those that curse them, as Joseph did to his brothers; and how they would strive to serve God and do good, as Joseph did in the court of Pharaoh. They would be full of love, too, to their fathers and brothers, as Joseph was to his.

How did Joseph get to be so good? By his trust in God and his prayers to Him. In all that came to him, be it bad or good, he saw the hand of God, and was full of love to Him through it all. Thus God blest him, as He does all who put their trust in Him.

CHAPTER XVI.

MOSES.

WHEN Joseph and all his brothers were dead, their sons and sons' sons grew to be more and more, till the land was full of them.

Now there rose up a new king in Egypt who knew not Joseph. And he said to the Egyptians, "Lo, these Hebrews are more than we are; let us be wise, and put them down, lest, if there should be a war, they might join our foes, and fight us, and so get off out of the land."

So they set men to rule them and make them work hard. And they made them build towns for Pharaoh. But the more they put them down, the more they grew. And the Egyptians were wroth to see them grow; so they made them serve more and more, till they were poor slaves, who had to toil hard night and day for their lords, and have poor fare, and small rest, and be beat when they did not work.

But still they grew, till at last Pharaoh made a law that all the Hebrew boys that were born should be thrown in the Nile. He let the girls live, but slew all the boys.

At that time one of the Hebrew mothers had a sweet child born, a boy; and when she saw he was so sweet, she could not bear to have him die; but she knew the Egyptians would come to throw him in the Nile. Poor mother! she hid her boy for three months, so that the men could not find him; and when she saw she could hide him no more, she made an ark of grass and reeds, and put slime and pitch on it, so as to keep it dry, and in it she put her babe, and laid it in the flags on the edge of the stream. Then she sent his sister to stand and watch, and see if he would be found there, and what would be done to him. The mother was not far off, we may be sure; it was so hard for her to go home and leave her dear babe there, and think that she had seen him for the last time. But she thought, "I will leave him to God, and to the stream and the sky, and will not let those bad Egyptians have him." While she wept for him, God saw the babe, and took care of him.

As the ark swung to and fro in the high reeds on the brink of the stream, and the babe slept as if he was in his mother's arms, Pharaoh's daughter came down with her maids to bathe in the stream; and as they were on the bank she saw the ark in the flags, and sent her maid to bring it to her. What could it be, put there so near the stream? When she saw the babe he wept, and she was sad at heart, and said, "Poor child! it is a Hebrew babe!"

As she took the child in her arms, his sister, who was close by, hid in the flags, took heart to come up to her, and said, "Shall I go and call to thee a Hebrew nurse, that she may nurse the child for thee?"

FINDING OF MOSES

And Pharaoh's daughter, whose heart was won by the sweet face of the child, all wet with tears, said she might go. So the sister went with joy and brought the child's mother.

And Pharaoh's daughter said to her; "Take this child and nurse it for me, and I will give thee thy hire." So the mother took the child, and bore it off to her home, with what joy of heart! No more, dear child, shalt thou be left by the lone stream, with the birds to hop round thee and look in thy face, and the frogs to sing close to thy bed; thou shalt sleep now on thine own mother's breast while she sings to thee the sweet songs of Israel!

Thus God took care of Moses—that was the babe's name, which Pharaoh's daughter gave to him, for the word Moses means "drawn out of the stream."

And the child grew, and his mother brought him to the king's daughter, and he was brought up in her house as her son. He was taught in all the books of the Egyptians, so that he knew a great deal more than if he had been brought up with the rest of the Hebrew boys, for they were now slaves, and could not learn much.

But when Moses was grown, he did not like to live in Pharaoh's court, wear fine clothes, and be at his ease, when all the rest of the Hebrews were slaves, ground down to the dust by the Egyptians, and made to toil so hard. Moses, too, had love for the God of his fathers, and it gave him no joy to live in the midst of those who knew not God, but had their false gods of wood and stone. He chose to bear pain and shame with the church of God, more than to have all the wealth of Egypt, and live as the son of Pharaoh's daughter, in the midst of the sins of the court; for he knew that God would bless the good, and bring the bad to shame at last. He had faith in God, and would give up all his wealth, if it was wrong to keep it.

So it came to pass, when Moses was a grown man, that he went to see his brothers, the Hebrew slaves, to see what he could do for them. As he found them at their toil, an Egyptian beat a Hebrew man; Moses ran to help his brother, and slew the Egyptian, and hid him in the sand.

The next day he saw two Hebrews

fight, and he went to try and make peace, and said to the one who was in the wrong, "Why dost thou smite thy brother?"

But the man said, "Who made thee a prince and a judge for us? Wilt thou kill me, as thou didst the Egyptian?"

Then Moses had fear, and said, "It is known that I slew the Egyptian." And when Pharaoh heard of it, he sought to slay Moses.

Then Moses fled from the court of Pharaoh. He thought he could do no good in Egypt. His brothers would not let him help them, so he could not do them good. He went off to the land of Midian, and when he got there, sad at heart, his feet sore with the hot sand of the way, he sat down to rest by a well, where there was a green spot and a few palm trees, in the midst of the sand.

Now there was a priest of Midian who had seven daughters, and they came and drew from the well, for their father's flock.

But some men came with their sheep, and drove them from the well. Then Moses stood up for them, and gave their flock drink. And when they came to their father, he said, "How is it that ye are come so soon this day?" And they said, "An Egyptian was at the well when the men drove us off, and he drew for us, and for the flock."

And their father said, "Where is he? Why is it that ye have left him? Call him, that he may eat bread."

So Moses came to the priest, and was with him a long time; and he gave him his daughter for his wife.

And it came to pass at that time that the king of Egypt died; but the Hebrew slaves grew worse and worse off, and their cries and groans went up to God. And God heard their groans, and thought of his word that he spake to Abraham, Isaac and Jacob; and he came to help them. For he hears the cry of the poor and the slave.

CHAPTER XVII.

THE BURNING BUSH.

Now Moses kept the flock of Jethro, his wife's father, the priest of Midian, and he led the flock to the back side of the field of sand, and came to the mount of God, to Horeb.

And the Lord came to him in a flame of fire out of the midst of a bush; and he saw, and lo! the bush was on fire, and yet it was not burnt.

And Moses said, " I will now turn, and see this great sight, why the bush is not burnt."

And when the Lord saw that he came to see, God spoke to him out of the midst of the bush, and said, "Moses, Moses." And he said, "Here am I."

And he said, "Come not near; put off thy shoes from off thy feet; for the place where thou dost stand is God's ground." And God said, "I am the God of thy father, the God of Abraham, the God of Isaac, and the God of Jacob."

And Moses hid his face, for he did not dare to look on God.

And the Lord said, "I have seen the grief of the Hebrews, whom I love, in Egypt, and have heard their cry, since they were made slaves. I know all their groans. And I am come down to free them out of the hand of the Egyptians, and to bring them up out of that land to a good land and a large, to a land that flows with milk and sweets, to the land of Canaan. Come now, and I will send thee to Pharaoh that thou mayst bring forth my sons, the Hebrews, out of Egypt."

And Moses said to God, "Who am I, that I should go to Pharaoh, and that I should bring forth a whole race out of Egypt?"

And God said, "I will be with thee; and this shall be a sign to thee, that I have sent thee; when thou hast brought them forth from Egypt, ye shall serve God on this mount."

And Moses said to God, "Lo, when I come to the Hebrews, and shall say to them, the God of your fathers hath sent me to you, and they shall say to me, 'What is his name?' What shall I say to them?"

And God said to Moses, "I AM THAT I AM. Thus shalt thou say to the Hebrews, I AM hath sent me to you. The Lord God of your fathers, the God of Abraham, the God of Isaac, and the God of Jacob, hath sent me to you. This is my name for all time, as long as the world shall last. Go, call the old men of Israel, and say to them, the Lord God of your fathers came to me, and said: I have been with you, and have seen that which is done to you in Egypt. And I have said, I will bring you up out of Egypt to the land of Canaan, to a land that flows with milk and food.

"And they shall hear thy voice, and thou shalt come, thou and the chief men of Israel to the king of Egypt, and ye shall say to him, the Lord God of the Hebrews hath met with us; now let us go, we pray thee, three days off in the plain, that we may pray and bring gifts to the Lord our God.

"And I am sure that the king of Egypt will not let you go, no, not by his great might.

"And I will stretch out my hand and smite Egypt with all my plagues which I will bring on the land; and then he will let you go. And I will make Israel great in the sight of the Egyptians; so that when ye go, ye shall not go poor, as ye are now; but the Egyptians shall lend you great store of gold and rich things; and ye shall spoil the Egyptians."

And Moses said, "But what if they should not trust me, nor hear my words? They will say, The Lord did not come to thee."

And the Lord said, "What is that in thine hand?" and he said, "A rod."

And he said, "Cast it on the ground." And Moses cast it on the ground, and it came to be a snake; and he fled from it.

And the Lord said to Moses, "Put forth thine hand, and take it by the tail." And he put forth his hand, and caught it, and it was a rod once more in his hand.

And the Lord said, "Show them this sign, that they may know that the Lord God of their fathers, the God of Abraham, the God of Isaac, and the God of Jacob, hath in truth come to speak to thee."

Then the Lord said to him, "Put

now thine hand in thy breast;" and he did so; and when he took it out, it was white with sores. And he said, "Put it in thy breast once more;" and Moses did so, and when he took it out, it was all well, like the rest of his skin.

And God said, "If they will not hear thee, when they have seen the first sign, then show them this one, and they will hear. But if they will not hear the two signs, then thou shalt take of the stream, and place it on the dry land; and what thou dost take from the stream shall turn to blood on the dry land."

But Moses still did not want to go, though God gave him such might to do signs, and he said, "Oh my Lord, I can not speak well; I am slow of speech and of a slow tongue."

And the Lord said to him, "Who hath made man's mouth; who doth make men deaf, or dumb, or blind? Do not I the Lord? Go, and I will be with thee, and teach thee what to say."

And Moses said, "Oh! my Lord, send, I pray thee, by the hand of some one else."

And the Lord was wroth with Moses, that he had not faith to go and trust that God would make all go right. And God said to him, "Is not Aaron thy brother? I know that he can speak well. He will soon come to meet thee, and when he sees thee, he will be glad in his heart. And thou shalt speak to him, and tell him what to say; and I will be with thee and with him, and will teach you what ye shall do. He shall speak for thee; thou shalt tell him God's will, and he shall tell it to the men of Israel. And thou shalt take this rod in thine hand, to do signs with."

So Moses went back to Jethro, a new man. He was to keep sheep no more, but was to rule the men of Israel, and bring them out of their bonds. All that he knew in his youth in Pharaoh's court would now come to use, to fit him to lead Israel; and the years he had spent in the wilds with Jethro were not lost, for there he had had time to think and pray.

But now he must act; so he said to Jethro, "Let me go back, I pray thee, to my brothers in Egypt, and see if they yet live." And Jethro said to him, "Go in peace."

And the Lord spake to him once more, and said, " Go, for all the men are dead that sought thy life."

And Moses took his wife and his two sons, and set them on a mule, and set forth to go to Egypt; and he took the rod of God in his hand.

And the Lord said to Aaron, " Go out in the wood to meet Moses." And he went and met him in the mount of God, and gave him a kiss of love. And Moses told Aaron all the words of the Lord who had sent him, and all the signs which he had told him of.

And Moses and Aaron went to all the chief men of Israel; and Aaron told them all the words which the Lord had told Moses, and did the signs in their sight. And the people had faith in them, and when they heard that the Lord had seen their grief, and had come down to help them, then they bent down their heads and gave thanks to him.

Then Moses and Aaron went in and told Pharaoh, "Thus saith the Lord God of Israel; let Israel go, that they may hold a feast to me in the plain."

And Pharaoh said, "Who is the Lord, that I should hear his voice to let Israel go? I know not the Lord, nor will I let Israel go."

And they said, "God hath sent us to thee; and let us go we pray thee, three days off on the plain, and take gifts to the Lord our God."

And the king of Egypt said to them, "Why do ye, Moses and Aaron, keep the men from their work; get you to your task? Lo, the land is full of Hebrews, and ye make them stop their work."

And Pharaoh said the same day to the men who had the care of the Hebrew slaves, "Ye shall no more give them straw to make brick of, as ye have done; let them go and pick up straw. And ye shall make them do just as much as when they had straw; ye shall not take it off from them at all; for they do not want to work, and so they cry, 'Let us go and serve our God.' Let there be more work laid on the men, that they may have no time to hear vain words."

So the task men went out and spoke to the Hebrews, and said, "Thus saith Pharaoh, I will not give you straw. Go ye, get your straw where you can find it; yet you must do all your work."

So they went to and fro through the land of Egypt, to pick up chips and sticks to use for straw. And the task men drove them, and said, "Do your work, your task for each day, as when there was straw." And when they could not do it, they beat them, and said, "Why do ye not do your task and make your brick, as you did once?"

Then the chief men of Israel came and said to Pharaoh, "Why dost thou deal thus with thy slaves? They give us no straw, and yet they say to us, make brick, and then they beat us; but the fault is theirs, not ours."

But he said, "You do not want to work; so ye say, let us go and serve our God. Go and work; ye shall have no straw, and yet ye must make brick."

The men of Israel were in a sore plight—told to do work which they could not. And when they met Moses and Aaron, who stood in the way as they came out from Pharaoh, they said, "The Lord look on you and judge if ye have done right; ye have made Pharaoh and his men hate us, and have put a sword in their hand to slay us."

And Moses could not say a word to them, he was so hurt in his soul. But he went to the Lord, and said, "Lord, why hast thou done so to these men? Why is it that thou hast sent me? For since I have come to Pharaoh to speak in thy name, he has done harm to Israel; and thou hast not set them free at all."

The Lord did not blame Moses that his heart was so sad, but gave him strength, and said to him, "Now shalt thou see what I will do to Pharaoh; for with a strong hand shall he let them go, and shall drive them out of his land. I am the Lord. I came to Abraham, to Isaac, and to Jacob, and I gave them my word that I would give them the land of Canaan, the land where I had led them to dwell. I have heard the groans of Israel, whom the Egyptians have made slaves; and I have thought on my word that I spake. Now say to Israel once more, 'I am the Lord; I will bring you out from the hand of the Egyptians, with my strong arm; I will take you to be mine, and I will be to you a God; and ye shall know that I am the Lord your God, which brought you out of Egypt. And I will bring you to the land, which I did swear to give to Abraham, Isaac and Jacob; I will give it to you to be your own; I am the Lord.'"

And Moses spake these words to Israel; but they heard him not, for grief of heart, and for hard toil and bonds.

Chapter XVIII.

THE TEN PLAGUES.

And God said to Moses, "Co to Pharaoh, and tell him to send Israel out of his land. But his heart will be hard till I have made him see my signs in the land of Egypt. He will not hear you, and I will lay my hand on Egypt, and bring Israel forth with great signs; that the Egyptians may know that I am the Lord."

And Moses and Aaron did as the Lord told them. Moses was four score years old, and Aaron four score and three, when they went in to Pharaoh. And the Lord told Moses,

"When Pharaoh shall say, 'Show me a sign,' then thou shalt say to Aaron, 'Take thy rod, and throw it down,' and it shall turn to a snake."

And he did so; Aaron threw down his rod, and it was a snake. Then Pharaoh told his wise men to do the same thing, and they did; but Aaron's rod ate up their rods. Then Pharaoh would not hear them, as the Lord had said.

And the Lord said to Moses, "Pharaoh's heart is hard, he will not let them go. Go to him at morn, when he goes out to the stream, and stand by the bank till he shall come; and take thy rod in thine hand. And thou shalt say to him, 'The Lord God of the Hebrews hath sent me to thee, and hath said, Let Israel go, that they may serve me; and thou wilt not hear Thus said the Lord, 'Now shalt thou know that I am the Lord; lo, I will smite with the rod that is in my hand on the stream, and it shall turn to blood. And the fish that are in it shall die, and the stream shall be so foul, that no one can drink of it.'"

And Moses and Aaron did so; Aaron took the rod, and smote the stream, in the sight of Pharaoh and his court; and all the stream was full of blood, and there was blood in all the ponds and pools through all the land of Egypt, so that they could not drink; and they had to dig new wells to drink from.

But still Pharaoh's heart was hard; he would not do as the Lord said; he would not let Israel go. And the stream ran blood for seven days, sc that none could drink from it.

Then the Lord said to Moses, "Say to Pharaoh, if thou wilt not let Israel go, I will smite all the land with frogs; the streams shall bring forth frogs, and they shall go up and come to thine house, and to thy bed, and shall be in thy food and through all thine house and through the whole land." And Aaron put forth his rod, and the frogs came out of the streams and ponds, and went all through the land.

Then Pharaoh sent for Moses and Aaron, and said, "Pray to the Lord, that he may take the frogs out of the land; and I will let Israel go."

And Moses, "I will; and thou shalt know that there is none like to the Lord our God. The frogs shall gc from thee and thy house, and from all the land. So Moses went to the Lord to ask Him to kill the frogs; and the Lord did as he said, and the frogs were all dead in each house and in the fields; and there were great heaps of them all through the land.

But when Pharaoh saw that they were gone, his heart was hard, and he would not let Israel go, as he had said he would.

And the Lord said to Moses, "Say to Aaron, stretch out thy rod, and smite the dust of the earth; and it shall breed lice through all the land."

And he did so, and there were lice on man and on beast. And Pharaoh's wise men said to him, "This is the hand of God;" but Pharaoh's heart was hard, and he would not hear them; as the Lord had said.

And the Lord said to Moses, "Rise up at the break of day, and go to Pharaoh, as he comes forth to the stream, and say to him, Thus saith the Lord; let Israel go, that they may serve me. If thou wilt not let them go, I will send swarms of flies on thee, and on thy land; it shall be full of flies. But in the land of Goshen, where Israel dwells, there shall be no flies; that thou mayst know that I am the Lord."

And the Lord did so, and there came swarms of flies all through the land, but not in Goshen.

And Pharaoh called for Moses and Aaron, and said, "You may serve God in this land." But they said, "No, it is not fit for us to do that; for we must have sheep and cows for our gifts to God, and we can not take them here, for they are the gods of the Egyptians, and they would stone us if we took their gods." (For the Egyptians made false gods of sheep and cows and bulls.) And they said, "We must go three days' off in the wild land, and serve God as He shall tell us."

And Pharaoh said, "I will let you go, if ye will not go far off. But pray to God to kill these swarms of flies."

And Moses said, "I will, but let not Pharaoh break his word, and hold Israel still in bonds."

So Moses went from Pharaoh, and put up a prayer to God to kill the flies; and God did so; they were all gone; there was not one left.

But Pharaoh's heart was still hard, and he would not let Israel go.

Then the Lord said to Moses, "Go to Pharaoh, and tell him, Thus saith the Lord God of the Hebrews, let them go, that they may serve me: for if thou wilt not let them go, lo, the hand of the Lord shall be on the beasts of the field, the flocks and the herds; they shall all be sick. But the flocks of the Hebrews shall be well; not one of them shall die." And the Lord said He would do this thing the next day.

And the next day the flocks of the Egyptians were all sick to death; but of the flocks of Israel not one was sick.

And when Pharaoh heard that the flocks of Israel were not sick, his heart was hard, and he would not let them go

And the Lord said to Moses and Aaron, "Take dust from the fire, and throw it up to the sky in the sight of Pharaoh, and it shall be a boil on man and on beast through all the land of Egypt." And he did so, and boils broke out on all in Egypt. But still Pharaoh's heart was hard, and he would not let Israel go.

Then the Lord said to Moses, "Go and tell Pharaoh, Let Israel go, that they may serve me. For if thou wilt not let them go, I will send all my plagues on thee and on thy land, that thou mayst know that there is none like me in all the earth. And I will smite thee and thy land with death; and thou shalt be cut off from the earth. Dost thou think thou art as strong as God? I will show thee and all the world how weak thou art, and that thou art a fool to set up thy will for mine. And now I will send a rain and hail, such as hath not been seen in Egypt; send and get in thy herds and all that thou hast in the field; for on man and beast that are found in the field and are not brought home, the hail shall come down, and they shall die."

Those that had fear of the word of the Lord made their slaves and their flocks flee to the house; but those that had no fear of the Lord left them out in the field. How strange that fear should not have been in the hearts of all to this great God, who had brought on them such sore plagues!

And the Lord said to Moses, "Stretch forth thy rod to the sky, that the hail may come!" And he did so; and the Lord sent hail and storm, and the fire fell from the clouds, and ran on the ground. Hail, and fire with the hail! there had been none like it in Egypt since the earth was made. And the hail smote man and beast, and the trees, and the plants of the field. But in the land of Goshen, where Israel dwelt, there was no hail.

And Pharaoh in great fear, sent for Moses and Aaron, and said, "I have done wrong this time; the Lord is just, and I and my house are bad. Oh, pray to God that the hail may stop! and I will let you go; ye shall stay no more."

And Moses said to him, "As soon as I am gone out of the town, I will spread forth my hands to the Lord, and the fire and hail shall cease; that thou mayst know that the earth is the Lord's. But as for thee and thy house, I know that ye will not yet fear the Lord God."

And Moses did so, and there was no more hail or rain. And when Pharaoh saw that the rain and the hail were gone, he did yet worse, and made his heart hard, he and his court. And he would not let Israel go, as the Lord had said to Moses.

And the Lord said to Moses once more, "Go to Pharaoh; I will show all my signs to him, that thou mayst tell thy sons, and thy sons' sons, what things I have done in Egypt; that ye may know that I am the Lord."

And Moses and Aaron came to Pharaoh, and said, "Thus saith the

Lord God, How long wilt thou not do as I say? Let Israel go, that they may serve me. If thou wilt not, lo! I will bring great bugs in the land, and they shall be so thick, that one can not see the earth, and they shall eat the rest of that which is left from the hail. And they shall fill thy house, and all the towns and the whole land. They shall be such as have not been seen on the earth till now."

And Moses went out from Pharaoh. And Pharaoh's court that stood round him, said, "How long shall this Moses bring plagues on us? Let the men go and serve the Lord their God. Dost thou not know that Egypt is spoilt?"

Then Pharaoh sent for Moses and Aaron to come back, and said to them,

"Go serve the Lord your God; but who are they that shall go?"

And Moses said, "We will go with our young and with our old, with our sons and our daughters, with our flocks and our herds; for we must hold a feast to the Lord."

And he said, "I will not let you go thus, all of you; look to it; for I will do you harm." And he drove them out of his sight.

And the Lord said to Moses, "Stretch out thine hand for the great bugs that they may come and eat all in the land that the hail hath left."

And Moses held up his rod, and the Lord brought an east wind on the land all that day and all that night; and the next day the east wind brought the great bugs, and they were on the face of the whole earth, so that the land was dark with them; and they did eat the herbs and plants, and all the fruit of the trees; so that there was no green thing left in all the land.

Then Pharaoh sent for Moses and Aaron in haste, and said, "I have done wrong in the sight of the Lord your God, and in your sight; now pray to the Lord your God, that he will take from me my sin, and rid me of this plague."

And Moses went and made a prayer to God. And the Lord brought a strong west wind, which took off the bugs, and cast them in the Red sea; there was not one left. But as soon as they were gone Pharaoh would not let Israel go.

And the Lord said to Moses,

"Stretch out thine hand to the sky, that it may be dark in all the land of Egypt." And Moses put forth his hand, and it grew dark, and it was pitch dark for three days in all the land. No man could see, or rise from his place for three days; but it was light where Israel dwelt.

Then Pharaoh sent for Moses and said, "Go ye, serve the Lord, and take your sons and daughters with you; but let your flocks and herds stay here."

But Moses said, "We must take our flocks with us; there shall not a hoof be left; for of them must we take to serve the Lord our God; we know not what we shall want for gifts to him, till we get there."

Then Pharaoh would not let them go, and he said to Moses, "Get thee from me; see my face no more; for in the day that thou shalt see my face thou shalt die."

And Moses said, "It is well; I will see thy face no more."

Chapter XIX.

THE PASSOVER—ISRAEL LEAVES EGYPT.

And the Lord said to Moses, "Yet one more plague will I bring on Pharaoh and on Egypt; then he will let you go; and when that time comes, he will thrust you out all at once. Speak now to Israel, and tell them to ask all they want of the Egyptians, of gold and rich things."

And the Lord gave Israel grace in the sight of the Egyptians. And Moses was a great man in the land of Egypt, for Pharaoh and all the Egyptians were in great fear of him.

And Moses said, "Thus saith the

Lord, In the night will I go through all Egypt, and all the first born in the land of Egypt shall die, from the first born of Pharaoh on his throne, to the first born of the slave, and all the first born of beasts. And there shall be a great cry through all the land; there was none like it, nor shall there be. But in Israel none shall die; that ye may know how that the Lord doth take care of Israel. Then shall the Egyptians come to me, and bow down to me, and say, get thee out, and all Israel with thee; and then I will go."

And the Lord spake to Moses and Aaron, and said, "This month shall be the first month of the year to you; speak to all Israel and say, on the tenth day of this month each man shall take a lamb, one lamb for each house, and keep it four days; and on the fourth day they shall kill it, and they shall take the blood, and strike it on the two side posts and on the dooı post of the house where they shall eat it. And they shall eat the flesh in that same night, roast with fire. And thus shall ye eat it; with your clothes all on, your shoes on your feet, and your staff in your hand, as though you would start off at once. For I will pass through the land of Egypt this night, and will smite all the first born in the land of Egypt; I am the Lord. And the blood shall be for a sign on each house; and when I see the blood I will pass by you, and the plague shall not come on you, in that night when I smite the land of Egypt with death.

"And ye shall keep this day a feast

to the Lord as long as ye and your sons shall live."

Then Moses did call all the chief men of Israel and said to them, "Take a lamb each one of you for his house, and kill it; and put some of the blood of the lamb on the door of your house; none of you must go out at the door of his house through the night.

"For the Lord will pass through the land to smite the Egyptians, and, when he sees the blood on the door, he will pass by you, and will not let the plague come in to your house to smite you.

"Ye shall keep this day as a feast for you and your sons when ye are come to the land which the Lord will give you. And when your sons ask you, What mean you by this feast? ye shall say, It is the Lord's Pass-over, for he did pass by Israel on that night when he smote the Egyptians, and when he saw the blood of the lamb on the house, he would not let the plague come in to hurt us."

Then the men of Israel bent down their heads and gave praise to God. And they went each man to his house, and did as the Lord had told them.

They had faith in what God said, so they went in haste to put the blood of the lamb on their door posts to save them from the plague. God kept the plague from them when he saw the blood of the lamb, just as he will save us, for the sake of the blood of Christ, who is the Lamb of God slain for us. As the lamb died for the Hebrews, so God sent his own dear Son to die for us. So that if we put our trust in Christ we need not die for our sins, but may live with God in the skies, in great joy.

How good God was, to send his son to die for us! How good Christ was, to shed his blood on the cross, to save us from the plague of sin! Our sins would have made our hearts so bad that we must have been lost, if it had not been that Christ took them all on him, and died in our place, just as the plague would have been on the Hebrews, if it had not been for the blood of the lamb on their door posts. Christ is our lamb. Do we love him who has thus shed his blood for us?

It came to pass, in the same night when the lamb was slain, that the Lord smote all the first born in the land of Egypt, from the first born of Pharaoh that sat on his throne, to the first born of the slave that was in jail; and all the first born of beasts.

And Pharaoh rose up in the night, he and all his court, and all the Egyptians; and there was a great cry in Egypt; for there was not a house where there was not one dead.

And he sent for Moses and Aaron by night, and said, "Rise up, and get you forth out of my land, ye and all Israel, and go, serve the Lord, as ye have said. Take your flocks and your herds, as ye have said, and be gone; and bless me too."

And the Egyptians made haste, that they might send them out of the land; for they said, "We be all dead men."

And the Hebrews took their dough

with no yeast in it, and their bread pans they bound up in their clothes on their backs; and they did as Moses said, and took of the Egyptians, gold, and rich things and fine clothes. The Lord gave them grace in the sight of the Egyptians, so that they gave them all they did ask; and they took so much that they were now rich, and not poor.

So Israel went forth from Egypt, the land where they had been slaves for four hundred and thirty years. Oh! how glad they were to go and be free. There were six hundred thousand men, and a great crowd of wives and children; and large flocks and herds. They went forth that night, the hosts of the Lord; it is night much to be thought of, that night when the Lord brought his hosts out of Egypt.

God led them not through the land of the Philistines, though that was a near way to Canaan; for He said; "If they should see war in the land of the Philistines, they might fear, and want to go back to Egypt." So he led them by the way of the sands of the Red Sea.

And Moses took the bones of Joseph with him; for Joseph had said, "God will be sure to come and bring you back to Canaan; and ye shall take my bones with you."

And the Lord went in front of the host in a dark cloud, by day, and in a bright cloud of fire by night, to show them the way. By day and by night, the Lord was with them, to guide and to keep them.

Chapter XX.

THE RED SEA.

When Pharaoh saw that the Hebrews had fled, his heart grew hard once more, and he said to his court, "Why have we done this, to let our slaves go? Let us go and catch them, and bring them back."

So he set forth with a great host of men of war, and went as fast as he could in the track of the Hebrews; and he came up with them in their tents by the Red Sea.

As Pharaoh came nigh, the Hebrews did look, and lo! the Egyptians came on them; and they were in great fear, and made a great cry to the Lord. And they said to Moses, "Were there no graves in Egypt, that thou hast brought us here to die in these sands? Why hast thou brought us out of Egypt? Is not this the word that we told thee, to let us be, that we might serve the Egyptians? We wish we were still slaves, and had not come out here to die!"

How soon did their faith in God leave them! Could they not trust Him, who had done so much for them, and was with them now in the bright cloud?

And Moses said to them, "Fear not; stand still, and see how the Lord will save you this day; for the Egyptians whom ye have seen this day, ye shall see no more. Be still, and the Lord will fight for you."

Then the Lord said to Moses, "Why dost thou cry to me? Speak to Israel, that they go on. Lift thou up thy rod, and stretch out thine hand to the sea, and Israel shall go on dry ground through the midst of the sea."

And now the cloud that had been in front of the Hebrews, went and stood at their back, to keep them from the Egyptians; it made the camp of the Egyptians all dark, but it gave light through the night to Israel; so Pharaoh came not near them all that night.

Then Moses put out his hand to the sea; and the Lord made the sea go back by a strong east wind all that night, so that there was dry land in the sea; and Israel went through the midst of the sea on dry ground; the waves were a wall to them on their right hand and on their left.

And the Egyptians went in to catch them in the midst of the sea, all Pharaoh's men of war. But the Lord did look on the host of the Egyptians out of the cloud of fire, and made them to fear, and took off the wheels from their cars, so that they could not drive; and they said, "Let us flee from the face of Israel; for the Lord fights for them."

Then the Lord said to Moses, "Stretch out thine hand to the sea, that the waves may come back on the Egyptians."

Moses put forth his hand to the sea; and the sea came back in its strength as the sun rose; and the Egyptians fled from it; but the Lord cast them down in the midst of the sea; and the waves came back on Pharaoh and all his host; there was not one of them left. But Israel went on dry land in the midst of the sea; and the waves were a wall for them on their right hand and on their left.

Thus the Lord took Israel that day out of the hand of the Egyptians, and Israel saw the Egyptians dead on the sea shore. They saw the great work which the Lord did on the Egyptians; and they were in fear of the Lord, and had faith in Him and in Moses.

Then they all sang a song of praise to the Lord. Miriam, the sister of Aaron, gave praise to the Lord in a song and a dance; and all sang with her for joy.

CHAPTER XXI.

THE WILDERNESS.

WHEN Moses had brought Israel through the Red Sea, they went on in the wild waste of sand, and for three days they found no water.

Then the whole host had great thirst, and when they came to Marah, a place where there was a well, they were all glad, for they thought now they could drink. But when they came to taste of the spring, lo! it was not good, and no man or beast could drink of it. Then they found fault with Moses, just as though he could help it, and said, "What shall we drink?"

They might have known that God would make it all right, but no, in their thirst they thought they should die, and they lost their trust in God.

Then Moses went to God, to ask Him what he should do, and the Lord told him to put a tree, that grew near by, in the stream; and when he had done this, it came to be sweet and good to drink, and all the host drank of it. I should think they would have felt shame, to think they could not put their faith in God to take care of them, when they knew He was so good, and so full of love and strength. God did not give them up for their want of faith, but spoke to them in great love, and said, "If ye will hear the voice of the Lord your God, and will do that which is right in His sight, and give ear to His words and keep them, I will put none of those plagues on you that I brought on the Egyptians; for I am the Lord that heals you."

Then they went on, and came to Elim, where there were twelve wells and three score and ten palm-trees, and they made their camp there by the wells. For in that great plain of sand and rocks where their way led them, a well and a few trees were a great joy to their eyes, and they were glad to rest in the shade of the trees.

At last all the host went on from Elim, and took their way through the great wild plain. It was now six weeks since they had left the land of Egypt.

The cloud of shade by day and of fire by night went with them, so that they knew God was there all the time to lead them. They ought to have been glad to go where He thought it best to take them, though it was through the hot sand and not through green fields; but no, when they saw how dry and hot it was, they all with a loud voice found fault with Moses and Aaron, just as though it was they and not God, who had brought them there; and they said, "Would to God we had died by the hand of the Lord in the land of Egypt, where we all had meat, and where we did eat bread to the full; for ye have brought us forth to these sands, to kill us all for want of bread."

How wrong this was, when God had told them He would lead and feed them. But God was still kind, and He said to Moses, "Lo, I will rain bread from the skies for you, and each man shall go out and pick up his share each day, that I may prove them, and see if they will walk in my law or not.

"And it shall come to pass that on the sixth day they shall cook that which they bring in; and it shall be twice as much on that day as on the rest of the days of the week."

Then Moses and Aaron said to all the host, "This night ye shall know that the Lord hath brought you out from the land of Egypt. In the morn, ye shall see the love and might of God. For He hath heard your words, how ye found fault with Him. And what are we that ye should speak so to us? It is not we that have brought you here, but God?"

And Moses said, "The Lord will give you at night meat to eat, and in the morn bread to the full, for He hath heard your hard words, that ye spake of Him, though He had been so good to you."

Then he said to Aaron, "Tell all the host to come near to the Lord."

And it came to pass, as Aaron spoke to the host, that they all saw the fire of the Lord in the cloud.

And the Lord said to Moses, "I have heard their hard words; speak to them, and say, At night ye shall eat flesh, and at morn ye shall have your fill of bread; and ye shall know that I am the Lord your God."

And it came to pass that night, that great flocks of quails, which are such nice birds to eat, came all round the camp; and in the morn the dew lay on the ground round the host; and when the dew was gone up, lo! on the face of the ground there lay a small round thing, as small as the hoar frost on the ground.

And when the Hebrews saw it, they said, "What can it be?" For they knew not what it was. But Moses said to them, "This is the bread which the Lord hath sent you to eat. This is the thing which the Lord hath said; let each man take his share, just so much for each; and let each man take for those that are in his tent."

Then they did so, and took, some more, some less, to feed all that were in their tents.

And Moses said, "Now ye have

all ye want for this day, but let no man try to keep it till the next day." Thus God taught Israel to trust him, and not to take thought for the next day.

Some of them would not mind Moses, and they tried to keep it. But they found it would not keep. It bred worms, and was bad.

So each day the bread fell from the skies with the dew, and they went out to pick it up; and when the sun grew hot, it would melt.

And it came to pass that, on the sixth day, they got twice as much for each man; and the old men of the host came and told Moses of it. And he said to them, "This is that which the Lord hath said; the next day shall be the good day of rest to the Lord; take your bread from the skies, and bake it or boil it this day; and that which is left lay up to use on the day of rest."

So they laid it up for the next day, as Moses bade them; and it did not grow bad, nor breed worms.

And Moses said, "Eat what ye have laid by this day; for this is the Lord's day of rest; and this day ye shall not find it in the field. Six days ye shall get it; but on the day of rest there shall be none."

And it came to pass, that some of the host had no faith in what God said to them by Moses; so they went out on the day of rest to get bread; but they found none.

Then the Lord said to Moses, "How long will ye break my word and my laws? Do ye not see that the

Lord gives you the day of rest, and on the sixth day he gives you the bread of two days; stay each man in his place; let no man go out of his place on the day of rest."

So Israel took a rest on the Lord's day.

This bread that came from the skies was like a small white seed, and its taste was sweet and nice. Was not God good to feed Israel with food from the skies? Would we not like to have him send us down food each day? Well, that is just what he does; he sends us our food just as much as he did to Israel. Does he not make the grain grow for our bread? Does he not feed the cows and sheep with nice grass, that they may give us milk and meat? We ought then to thank him for our food each time we eat, just as much as Israel each time they found their food on the ground with the dew.

Then Moses said, "This is the thing that the Lord says you must do; fill a pot with this bread from the skies, to be kept through all time; that your sons may see the bread with which I have fed you in the wilds, when I brought you forth from the land of Egypt."

And he said to Aaron, "Take a pot and put this bread in it, and lay it up to be kept."

So Aaron did as the Lord had said, and laid it up.

And the host of Israel fed on this bread two score years, till they came to the land of Canaan.

Then all the host went on their way, as the Lord told them to go, till they came to a place where they found no wells or springs to drink from. And in their thirst they chid with Moses, and said, "Give us to drink."

Then Moses said to them, "Why do ye blame me? Where is your faith in God? Why do ye thus try him with your want of faith? Can not he who gives you bread each day give you drink too?"

But they had great thirst, and they still found fault with Moses, and said, "Why is this that thou hast brought us up out of Egypt, to kill us all, and our flocks with thirst?"

And Moses said to the Lord, "What shall I do? The host will stone me, if I do not get them drink."

And the Lord said to Moses, "Go on in front, and take with thee the old men of Israel; and thy rod with which thou didst smite the stream take in thine hand. Lo, I will stand by thee there on the rock in Horeb, and thou shalt smite the rock, and there shall come out of it a stream, that all the host may drink."

And Moses did so in the sight of the old men of Israel. So the Lord gave drink to Israel, as he had brought them food, though they did not trust in him.

How apt we are to be cross, and find fault, if we can not have just what we want, as Israel found fault with Moses. When we are cross, it is God that we blame, for it is God who sends all things that come to us.

Shall we find fault with him? Is he not kind and good, and will he not do just what is best for us, as he did for those Hebrews? He leads us as he led them, though we do not see him.

Soon a host of men of the race of Amalek came to fight with the hosts of Israel. And Moses said to Joshua, "Choose some men, and go out and fight with Amalek, and I will stand on the top of the hill with the rod of God in my hand."

So Joshua did as Moses said, and fought with Amalek, and Moses Aaron, and Hur went up to the top of the hill.

And it came to pass, when Moses held up his hand, Israel put Amalek to flight, but when he let down his hand, Amalek beat Israel. Moses stood on the hill and held up his hands as long as he could, but at last he could hold them up no more; then they put a stone for him to sit on, and Aaron and Hur stood one on each side of him, and held up his hands all day long, till the sun went down. And Joshua beat the host of Amalek and drove them off. For God was on the side of Israel.

At that time Jethro, the priest of Midian, the father of Moses' wife, heard of all that God had done for him and for Israel, and how God had brought them out of Egypt. So Jethro took Moses' wife and his two sons, who had been with him all this time that Moses had led Israel out of Egypt, and he came with them to see Moses at his camp near mount Horeb.

Moses was glad to see them. He had left them to do what God told him, and now God brought them all back to him. If we give up things for God, he will give them back to us in this world or in the next.

CHAPTER XXII.

THE LAW OF GOD.

ISRAEL had now been three months on their way to Canaan when they came to the wild plain where mount Sinai is; and there they set up their tents in front of the mount.

And Moses drew near to God, and God spoke to him out of the mount, and said, "Thus shalt thou say to the house of Jacob, the host of Israel; Ye have seen what I did to the Egyptians, and how I have borne you on my wings of love, and brought you near to me. Now if ye will hear my voice, and do what I say, ye shall be to me my own race, that I love more than all the rest of the earth; (for all the earth is mine;) ye shall be near and dear to me Thus shalt thou say to them."

So Moses came and told them all these words. And they all said, "We will do what the Lord tells us to do."

And Moses brought back their words to the Lord, and the Lord said to him, "Lo, I will come to thee in a thick cloud, that all the host may hear when I speak to thee, and may know that I am with thee."

And the Lord said, "Go tell the host to be clean and pure, and to wash their clothes, and then to wait till the third day; for on the third day the Lord will come down in the sight of all the host, on mount Sinai. And thou shalt set bounds round the mount, and shalt say, Take care that ye go not up to the mount, or touch it at all; if ye touch the mount, ye shall be put to death.

"And when ye hear the trump sound long, then come near to the foot of the mount."

Then Moses went down from the mount, and told Israel all these things; and they did as the Lord had said.

And on the third day it came to pass, that there was a thick cloud on the top of the mount that sent forth fire, and smoke, and the loud sound of a trump was heard; so that all that were in the camp shook with fear.

Then Moses brought forth the host out of the camp to meet with God; and they stood at the foot of the mount. And Mount Sinai was all in a smoke, for the Lord came down on it in fire; the smoke of it went up as the smoke of a great flame, and the whole mount shook.

And when the voice of the trump kept on, and was more and more loud, God spake to Moses by a voice. And the Lord came down on the top of the mount, and spake to Moses to come up there; and Moses went up.

And the Lord said to Moses "Go down and charge Israel, lest they break through to the Lord to gaze, and die for their sin. Thou shalt come up, thou and Aaron with thee, but let not the rest of the host break through the bounds to come up to the Lord, lest they die."

So Moses went and told them these words.

Then the Lord spake out of the midst of the fire, and said, "I am the Lord thy God, that brought thee forth out of the land of Egypt, the house of thy bonds.

"Thou shalt have no gods but me.

"Thou shalt not make false gods like the things that are in the sky or in the earth or in the sea, to bow down to those things, or to serve them; for I, the Lord thy God, am a strict God, and will not bear those that hate me; but I will bless all that love me and keep my words.

"Thou shalt not take the name of the Lord thy God in vain; for the Lord will not bless those that take his name in vain.

MOSES AND THE TEN COMMANDMENTS

"Be sure to keep the day of rest, the Lord's day. Six days shalt thou work, and do all that thou hast to do, but the seventh day is the rest of the Lord thy God; in it thou shalt not do work, thou nor thy son nor thy daughter, thy man, nor thy maid, nor thy beasts, nor the guest that is in thy house. For in six days the Lord made the sky and the earth, the sea, and all that in them is, and he took the seventh day to rest; so the Lord blest that day, and made it his own.

"Love and serve thy father and thy mother; that thy days may be long in the land which the Lord thy God shall give thee.

"Thou shalt not kill.

"Thou shalt be pure in all thy thoughts and words and deeds.

"Thou shalt not steal.

"Thou shalt not say false words of any one.

"Thou shalt not want things that are not thine; thou shalt not long for thy brother's house, or his wife, or his man, or his maid, or his ox, or his ass, or any thing that is thy brother's."

These are the ten laws of God, that He spake from Mount Sinai. He spake them to all the world, as much as to Israel, and we must keep them all, for they are God's laws.

And all Israel saw the fire and smoke, and heard the trump of God. And when they saw it, they went and stood far off. And they said to Moses, "Speak thou with us, and tell us what God says, and we will hear, but let not God speak with us, lest we die."

And Moses said to them, "Fear not, for God has come to prove you, that ye may so fear Him as not to sin."

Then they stood far off, while Moses drew near to the thick cloud where God was. And God gave him laws for Israel, and he came down and told them all the words of the Lord, and they all said with one voice, "What the Lord hath said, we will do."

And the Lord said to Moses, "Come up once more to me in the mount, and be there; and I will give thee two blocks of stone, with the law on them which I have made; that thou mayst teach Israel."

And Moses went up to the mount to God, and the cloud was on the mount. The cloud was there six days, like fire on the top of the mount; and all Israel saw it. And Moses went up in the midst of the cloud; and he was in the mount two score days and two score nights.

And when God had told Moses His laws, He gave him two blocks of stone, with the law on them, to teach Israel.

But when the host of Israel saw that Moses was a long time in the mount, they went to Aaron, and said to him, "Come, make us gods, which shall go with us, for as for this Moses, the man that brought us up out of the land of Egypt, we do not know where he is."

Ah, what bad men, to do just what God had told them not to do, make false gods to bow down to!

And Aaron said to them, "Break off the gold ear rings which are in the ears of your wives, of your sons, and of your daughters, and bring them to me." Then they all broke off their gold ear rings and brought them to him.

And he took them, and made of them a calf of gold; and they said, "These be thy gods, O Israel, which brought thee forth out of the land of Egypt."

And Aaron built a heap of stones in front of the calf, and said to them, "Let us have a feast to the Lord."

So they rose up the next day and brought their gifts and laid them in front of the calf of gold, and then they sat down to eat and drink, and rose up to play.

But God saw them, and He said to Moses, "Go, get thee down; for thy race that thou hast brought out of the land of Egypt have grown bad; they have soon gone out of the way which I told them. They have made them a calf of gold, and now they bow down to it, and bring gifts, and say, "These are our gods, that brought us out of Egypt!"

And the Lord said to Moses, "I have seen this race of Israel, and lo! their hearts are hard. They do not love God, and now I will leave them, and I will make of thee and of thy house a race which shall be mine."

But Moses said, "O Lord! let not thy wrath wax hot to Israel, whom thou hast brought forth out of the land of Egypt with thy strong arm. Why should the Egyptians speak, and say, 'For harm God brought them out, to slay them on the wild hills, and to blot out their name from the earth?' Oh! think of Abraham, Isaac and Jacob, to whom Thou didst say, 'I will make thy seed as the stars, and I will give this land to them for all time.'"

And the Lord heard the prayer of Moses, and said that He would not leave Israel, but would still bless them, in spite of their sin.

Then Moses went down from the mount, and the two blocks of stone, with the law on them, were in his hand; the law was on both sides of the two great stones. It was the work of God, done by His own hand.

Joshua was at the foot of the mount, and met Moses there, and as they went to the camp, he heard a shout, and said to Moses, " There is a noise of war in the camp."

And Moses said, " It is not the noise of war, but the noise of those who sing, that I hear."

And it came to pass, that as soon as he came nigh to the camp, he saw the calf, and the dance round it; and his wrath was so hot, that he cast the two blocks of stone down on the ground, and broke them at the foot of the mount. And he took the calf that they had made, and burnt it in the fire, and ground it to dust, and put the dust in the drink of the host, and made them all drink of it.

And he said to Aaron, " What harm have they done to thee, that thou hast brought so great a sin on them ?"

Then Aaron said, "Let not the wrath of my lord wax hot. Thou dost know Israel, and how their heart is set on sin. They said to me, Make us gods to go with us, for as for this Moses, that brought us out of Egypt, we do not know where he has gone. And I said to them, 'Bring me your gold,' and they brought it, and when I had cast it in the fire, there came out this calf."

Aaron was a weak man. He let the crowd rule him and make him sin, and then he put off the blame on them.

Then Moses stood in the gate of the camp, and said, "Who is on the Lord's side? Let him come to me." And all the sons of Levi went to him.

And he said to them, "Thus saith the Lord God, 'Ye must take your swords, and slay some of these men who have done this great sin.'"

Moses did not fear to do this, though he knew that this great crowd of men might kill him if they chose. But they did not dare to touch him, for they knew the great God was with him.

Then the sons of Levi went through the camp, and slew three thousand men. God told them to do it, and oh, what grief there was in the camp, and how they did mourn as they saw what their sin had brought on them! They knew now that they must fear God. They need not fear the Egyptians, or any one else; but God they must fear, and must not sin any more.

The next day Moses said to them, "Ye have done a great sin, but I will go up to the Lord once more, and pray to Him to blot out your sin."

And Moses did pray to the Lord, and said, "O Lord! Israel hath done this great sin, and hath made them gods of gold, but, I pray Thee, blot out their sin; take them back to Thy grace and let me bear Thy wrath in their place."

But God said, "No; he who hath done the sin must bear the blame. Do thou go, and lead them to the place that I have told thee of, I will show thee the way, but I will not go up in the midst of the host; for Israel has a hard heart, and they will not do my will."

When the people heard these words, they did mourn. They took off all their fine clothes and their gold, and did mourn and weep at the foot of the mount.

And Moses took a tent, and set it far off from the camp, and made it the church of the Lord; and each one who would pray to God went out to this tent, which was far off from the camp.

And it came to pass, when Moses went out to this tent of God, that all the host stood, each man in his tent door, to look at Moses, till he had gone in the tent of God. And as Moses went in, the bright cloud came down, and stood at the door of the tent, and the Lord spake with Moses face to face, as a man speaks to his friend.

When all Israel saw the bright cloud stand in the door of the tent, they rose up, and gave praise to God; each man in his own tent door. They were so glad to see the bright cloud once more. Then Moses came back to the camp, but Joshua, a young man, was in the tent of God all the time, to take care of it.

And Moses said to the Lord, "Thou dost say to me, 'Lead Israel to Canaan;' but how can I go if the Lord will not go with us; we can not; we must stay here, if Thou wilt not go with us."

And the Lord said to Moses, "I have heard thy prayer. I will do this thing, for thou hast found grace in my sight, and I know thee by name."

Will God hear us, as He heard Moses, and will He do what we ask Him? Yes, He will, for He says in

His word, "Ask, and ye shall have; seek, and ye shall find."

Then the Lord said to Moses, "Make two blocks of stone like the first, which thou didst break, and I will write on them the words that were on those; and come to me on the top of Mount Sinai. No man shall come with thee; let no man be seen on all the mount, and let no flocks or herds feed there."

And Moses did so. He rose up at dawn, and went to the top of the mount, as the Lord had said, and took in his hand the two blocks of stone. And the Lord came down in the cloud, and stood with him there, and he heard a voice, which said, "The Lord, the Lord God, full of love, and grace, and truth; He will bear long with men, and will blot out their sins when they turn from them; but He will by no means bless those who will not love Him."

And Moses made haste and bent down to the earth in the sight of God; and he said, "If now I have found grace in Thy sight, O Lord! I pray Thee, go with us, though we have such hard hearts; yet blot out our sins, and keep us for Thine own."

Moses did not ask that he might be blest, or his sons. His heart was not set on his own good, but on Israel; his prayer was for them.

And the Lord said, "I will go with Israel, and I will bring them to Canaan, and will drive out of the land all those who are there, that Israel may dwell there. For those who live there now are so bad, that ye must not go with them, or have any thing to do with them."

Moses was there with God two score days and two score nights. He did not eat or drink, for God gave him strength. And he wrote on the blocks of stone the ten laws of God.

Israel did not turn from God this time, though Moses was gone just as long as he was the first time. They had learnt not to make false gods.

And it came to pass, when Moses came down from Mount Sinai with the two blocks of stone in his hand, he had been with God so long, that the skin of his face shone; but he did not know it. And when Aaron and all Israel saw Moses, his face shone so that they did not dare to come near him. But Moses told them to come near, and he put a veil on his face, while he told them all the laws that God had told him.

When Moses went in to the Lord to speak with Him, he took the veil off, but when he came out to Israel, to tell them the word of God, his face shone so much, that he had to put it on.

Chapter XXIII.

THE HOUSE OF GOD.

Then Moses said, "Thus saith the Lord, 'All who love me, and would like to give to the Lord, may bring gifts to make my House fair and good. Bring fine cloth, and goats' hair, and red skins of rams to make the tent, and cloth to hang up for a door, and nice wood to make the boards, and bars, and pins, to set it up with. Then bring wood to make the ark of the Lord, and to make stands for the lights, and for the lambs who are slain for your sins. And bring gold to put on all these things. Bring, too, oil for the light, and spice to burn for a sweet smell. Let each one bring what he can.' "

And all Israel went from Moses to see what they could give, they all felt so glad to give to the Lord, and show Him that they meant to love Him. So they brought with a good will all the gold they had, and each one who had fine cloth or skins, brought them.

And all the wives that were wise did spin with their hands, and brought that which they had spun, fine cloth of all hues. And they spun goats' hair. The chief men brought stones, and spice and oil. So they all brought their gifts to the Lord, and were glad to work for Him.

And Moses said to them, "See, the Lord hath made one man, Bezaleel, wise in all kinds of work, to work in gold, and brass, and stones and wood, to cut stones and set them, and to carve wood. And He hath put it in his heart to teach you all how to work."

So all the men who knew how to work, with Bezaleel at their head, went to work on the house of the Lord. And Israel brought so much stuff to work with, that they had more than they could use.

And Bezaleel made the ark of fine wood, and put pure gold on all sides of it, and made a crown of gold round it; and he made for it four rings of gold, two on each side. And he made staves of wood with gold on them. And he put the staves in the rings, to lift the ark up with. And he put a sheet of pure gold on the top of the ark—the name of it was the seat of grace; and he made two angels of gold, and put one on each side of the seat of grace. They spread out their wings on high, to guard the seat of grace.

At last the work was all done, and they brought the tent and all the things with it to Moses. It was rich with gold and stones, and bright cloth; they had made it just as the Lord told Moses. And Moses did look on all their work that they had done for the Lord, and he blest them.

And the Lord spake to Moses, and said, "On the first day of the first month thou shalt set up the house of the Lord. And thou shalt put in it the ark, and put up the veil in front of the ark. And thou shalt bring in the stand, and set on it the things that are to be there; and thou shalt bring in the lamps and light them. And thou shalt set the gold stand on which the sweet spice is to be burnt, in front of the ark, and thou shalt hang the door of the tent. And thou shalt set the stand on which the lambs are to be slain and burnt in front of the door of the tent. And out side of the tent thou shalt set the stand where the priests are to wash. Then thou shall set up the fence of the court round it all, and hang up the door at the court gate.

"And thou shalt take the oil, and put it on the tent and all that is in it, to show that is the Lord's.

"And thou shalt bring Aaron and his sons to the door of the tent, and wash them, and put on them the priest's clothes, and put oil on them, that they may serve in my house; for they shall be the priests of the Lord."

Thus did Moses, all that God said to him he did. So the work was done, and the house of God set up.

Then the bright cloud of the Lord came down, and the house of the Lord was full of it; so that Moses could not go in; for the Lord was there.

And when the cloud went up from off the tent, then Israel went on their way; but when the cloud was on the tent, then they knew they were to rest. For the cloud of the Lord was on the tent by day, and the fire was on it by night, in the sight of all the house of Israel; in all their way.

Thus God was in His church, and

led His flock. And so He is now. We do not see Him in a cloud, but we see Him in Christ our Lord, who was on the earth so long. We do not burn sweet spice, but we put up our prayers, and they float up to God, as the smoke did. We do not slay lambs, but Christ was slain for us, and His blood blots out our sins. We have no ark, where God has His seat of grace, and where the priest must go and take the blood of the lamb, and pray for our sins, but we may go to God in our own house, or in the church, and then we find Him near to us, and ask Him to wash out our sins for the sake of the blood of Christ.

Since Christ came, we do not need all these things, for He brought God close to us. Israel had to come to

God through all these signs, for Christ had not come then, and they had to look on and hope He would come by and by. But now He has come, and God dwells with us, in each one of our hearts.

Then God gave Moses laws for all Israel, while they were still at the foot of Mount Sinai. He told him to count all the men of Israel, that were more than a score of years old, and could go forth to war, and see how large each tribe was. There were twelve tribes, of the twelve sons of Jacob. And Moses chose one man out of each tribe, to be the head and prince of the tribe, and to help him count the tribe. And they found there were more than six hundred thousand men in Israel who could go to war.

They did not count the tribe of Levi, for God chose that tribe to take care of His house, and be His priests, and they were not to go to war. They took care of the tent of God, and of all the things in it. When Israel went on their way, the Levites took down the tent of God, and bore it and all its things in front of the host; and when it was time for Israel to stop, then the Levites set up the tent of God and put the things in it; and no one else could touch it.

So Israel went on, each tribe in its own ranks, with its own prince, and its own camp by night. The house of God went with them in the midst of the tribe that took care of it, and the cloud of God did rest on it. Though they were in the wilds, far from all men, yet they were blest, for God was with them, and took such kind care of them. We are like them, for we, too, are on our way to our home. Our rest is not here, but in the skies, and we are on our way there, just as Israel were on their way to Canaan. God goes with us to show us the way. He feeds us and loves us, and will bring us at last to our home, if we but trust Him and go with Him, and do not stray off from Him.

When the cloud went up from the tent of the Lord, then Israel went on; but when it was at rest on the tent, then they set up their tents, and took rest; if it was two days, or a month, or a year, they were still, just as long as the cloud was still; and when the cloud went on, then they went on.

Shade by day, and light by night, a guide and a guard all the time, was the cloud of the Lord to Israel.

They were a whole year in the plain at the foot of Mount Sinai; but at the end of that time the cloud went up from the tent of the Lord, and led them on their way, for three days. The ark went first; and as the priests took it up to bear it in front of the host, Moses said, "Rise up, Lord, and let thy foes be put down; let them that hate thee flee." And when the cloud came down, and the ark had rest, he said, "Come back, oh Lord, to the hosts of Israel."

But Israel would not trust the Lord and love him all the time. They once more went back in their hearts to Egypt, and would long for the nice things they had to eat there, though they knew that God would soon take them to Canaan, their own fair land, if they would but have faith in him. They said, "We want more things to eat; we think of the meat and the roots and the herbs and the fruits that we had in Egypt; but now we do not have them, at all; we just have this bread from the sky, and we do not like it."

And Moses heard them weep for more food, each man in his tent door. He knew God would be wroth with them who would not trust him, and eat what he chose to give them, and Moses was sad, and sick at heart. He said to the Lord, "I can not lead Israel. They cry to me, Give us meat, that we may eat. What shall I do?"

And the Lord said to him, "Take three score and ten of the old men of Israel, and I will give them grace and make them wise, that they may help thee to lead Israel. And say to the host, I have heard your words, when ye said, who shall give us meat to eat, it was well with us in Egypt; and I will give you meat, that ye may eat. Ye shall have meat for a whole month. But ye shall not be blest when ye eat it, for ye have lost your faith in God, and found fault with him."

And Moses said, "Where shall meat come from to feed this great host? Shall the flocks and herds be slain for them, or shall the fish of the sea be all brought here for them?"

And the Lord said, "Has my arm lost its strength? Thou shalt see now if my word shall come to pass or not."

And Moses went out from the tent of the Lord, where God spoke to him, and told the hosts all these words. And he brought three score and ten old men to the tent of God, as God had told him. And the Lord came down in a cloud, and spake to him, and gave to these old men the same grace that Moses had, that they might know the will of God, and teach the host as he did. Thus God was kind to Moses, and set these men to help him.

And there were two men in the camp, on whom God sent his grace at the same time, and they spake his word too. Then a young man ran and told Moses of it; and Joshua said, " My lord Moses, shall we tell them not to do it? But Moses said, " Not so; I am glad they have this grace; would to God that all the host of Israel could preach too, and that God would put his word in them."

Moses would have been glad to have all Israel as great and as near to God as he was. He was glad when God put His grace in their hearts. He did not care to be first, but his sole thought was to do good.

Then there went out a wind from the Lord, and brought quails from the sea, and let them fall by the camp, on all sides as far as you could go in a day. They lay in heaps, and the host went out to get them, all that day and night, and all the next day; and they all had as much as they could eat.

But though they had their wish, the wrath of God came down with it, for they had done wrong to long for meat when He had not thought best to give it to them. A great plague came on them, and those who had said they must have meat, were sick and died.

This taught them that they must not weep and long for what God did not see fit to give them. He knew the bread from the sky was just the right food for them in the wilds, and that meat was not.

Do we wish and long for what we have not got? We must not do so, for God sees what is best for us, and if we had the thing we long for, how do we know but that it would harm us, as the quails did Israel? Let us trust

God, and be sure He gives us just what is right for us to have.

Aaron and Miriam, the brother and sister of Moses, thought that they could be as great as Moses, so they said, "God spake to Moses, but He spake to us, too, and told us to lead Israel." They were full of pride, but Moses was so meek, he did not care for self. All his thought was for Israel.

Then the Lord spake all at once to Moses, Aaron and Miriam, and said, "Come out ye three to the tent of the Lord." And they came out.

And the Lord came down in the cloud, and stood in the door of the tent, and said to Aaron and Miriam, "Hear now my words. If there be a seer in Israel, I will speak to him in a dream; but I will not speak so to

Moses; he takes care of my hosts, and is near to the Lord; with him will I speak mouth to mouth; my word shall be plain to him, and not in dreams. Why, then, do ye not fear to speak ill of Moses?"

And the wrath of the Lord was on them for this sin to their brother; and when the cloud went up, they saw that Miriam's skin was white with sores; she was so sick.

And Aaron said to Moses "Ah! my lord, let not this sin be on us; we have done wrong, but let her not be as one dead."

And Moses went to God, and said, "Heal her now, O Lord! I pray Thee."

And the Lord said, "She shall be sick and shut out from the camp seven days, lest she make the rest sick, then she shall get well."

So Miriam was shut out seven days, and had time to think of her sin, and to make up her mind that she would not try any more to put down Moses, and stand in his place.

The host did not move till Miriam was brought back to the camp. Then they went on their way.

Chapter XXIV.

THE SPIES—ISRAEL SHUT OUT FROM CANAAN.

Israel had now come near to the good land of rest—the land of Canaan. And the Lord spake to Moses, and said, "Send some men, that they may search the land of Canaan, which I will give to Israel; send one chief man from each tribe, to see the land."

So Moses sent a head man from each tribe to spy out the land of Canaan, and said to them, "Go this way, south, up to the hills, and see what the land is, and who live there, and if they be strong or weak; and what the land is that they dwell in, if it be good or bad, and if they live in towns, or tents, or in strong holds, and if the land is fat or lean, and if there be woods in it. Fear not; be brave, and bring us some of the fruit of the land."

Now it was the time of the first ripe grapes.

So they went up, and went through the land; and on their way back they came to a brook, and cut down from there a branch with one bunch of grapes; and it was so large, that it took two men to bring it on a stick; and they brought figs, too, and fruits.

And they came back in two score days. And when they had come to Moses, and Aaron and all the host, they gave them the fruit of the land; and they said, "We came to the land to which thou didst send us, and it is full of milk and food, and this is the fruit of it. But the men are strong that dwell in the land, and the towns have walls, and are strong; the men, too, are large and tall."

Then Caleb, one of the spies, told the rest to be still, and said, "Let us go up at once, and take the land; for we are strong, and can do it."

But the men that went up with him, said, "We can not go up; for the men there are more strong than we. They are so tall and big, that we look small in our own sight and in their sight."

Then all the host of Israel wept that night with loud cries; and they found fault with Moses and Aaron, and said, "Would to God we had died in the land of Egypt, or in the wild plain! Why has the Lord brought us to this land, to fall by the sword, and to be a prey to these men? let us go back to Egypt!"

Then Moses and Aaron were so cut to the heart, that they fell down on the ground in front of the host.

And Joshua and Caleb, two of the men that had been to search the land, rent their clothes with grief, and spoke to all the host, and said, "The land that we went through, is a good and a rich land; if we trust in the Lord, He will bring us to this land and give it to us, this fair land that flows with milk and sweets. But do not find fault with the Lord, nor fear the men of that land. They can do us no harm; their strength is gone from them; and the Lord is with us; fear them not." And all the host said they would stone Caleb and Joshua for these words.

Then the cloud came down on the tent of the Lord in the sight of all Israel. And the Lord said to Moses, "How long will this house of Israel sin? how long will it be ere they trust me, for all the signs which I have done for them? Though I have done all these signs for them, they put no faith in my word when I tell them I will give them this land of Canaan. Mind, now, I will have them no more for my house, but I will make of thee and thy house a race more great than they."

And Moses said to the Lord, "The Egyptians will hear it, and they will tell it to this land; for they have heard how Thou, Lord, art with Israel; that Thou, Lord, art seen face to face; that Thy cloud stands by them; that Thou dost go with them in the cloud, to give them shade by day and light by night. Now if Thou shalt kill all this house of Israel as one man, those that have heard the fame of Thee, will say, the Lord could not bring this race to the land which He sware to them, and He hath slain them in the wilds. Now, I pray Thee, let Thy grace be great, as Thou hast said, 'The Lord will bear long with men, and in His great love will blot out their sins.' Oh! blot out the sin of Israel this time, as Thou hast done all the way since we left Egypt till now."

And the Lord, He who hears the prayer of faith and love, heard Moses, and said to him, "I have done as thou dost pray. As I live, all the earth shall know the name of the Lord. But all these men of Israel which have seen my cloud and my fire, and all my signs which I did in Egypt and in the wild plain, and yet have not put their faith in me, nor heard my voice, they shall not see the land which I sware to their fathers; none of these that have found fault with God, and would not put their trust in me, shall see it. But Caleb, the one who had faith in me, and told them I would give them the land, he shall see the good land, and his seed shall dwell there. Now turn you, and get you back to the wild plain, by the way of the Red Sea."

And the Lord spake still to Moses and Aaron, and said, "How long shall

I bear with these bad men, who speak ill of their God? I have heard them all as they found fault with God, the God who hath led and blest them so long, and hath now brought them to the edge of the land of Canaan.

"Say to them, as I live, saith the Lord, as ye have said, so will I do to you. Ye had no faith when I told you I would bring you to your good land of Canaan, and now ye shall not see it. Ye shall die in the wilds; all this host that Moses did count, that were a score of years old and more, all those that would not put their trust in me, shall die. None shall see the good and, save Caleb and Joshua, who put their faith in my word, and were sure that I would do as I said, and drive out the men of Canaan to give you the land

"But your little ones, that ye said should be a prey, them will I bring in, and they shall know the land which ye would not take.

"Ye shall all go up and down in the wild plain two score years, till all are dead that have done this great sin. I will not bring Israel to the good land of Canaan for two score years more. And ye shall know that I am the Lord."

Then the spies, who went to search the land, and came back full of fear, and made all Israel to fear, were struck by the plague, and died. But Caleb and Joshua, the good men who had put their faith in God to drive out the men of Canaan, and to give them the land, were not sick at all.

And when Moses told the host of

Israel all the words of the Lord, they did mourn and weep.

And they rose up at dawn the next day, and went to the top of the hill, and said, "Lo! we are right near to the land of Canaan. We will go up and take it, for the Lord said He would give it to us."

And Moses said, "Why do ye now sin more? Go not up; for the Lord is not with you. Ye will fail, and be put down by the men of Canaan. Ye shall fall by the sword; for ye have gone from the Lord, and He will not be with you."

But they still thought they could go in their own strength. So up they went with a bold face to the top of the hill. But the ark of the Lord and Moses went not out of the camp.

Then the men of Canaan that dwelt on the hill, came on them, and smote them, and put them to flight; so that they fled, and left some of their men dead on the hill. And they all came back to the camp, and there they wept, and were sad. They were close by the land of Canaan, but God would not bring them in. They had had great fear of the men of Canaan, and no faith that God could give them the land, and now they could not have it, but must die in the wilds.

Oh, what a sad fate for these poor men, to see the land and not go to it! Now when it was too late, they saw what fools they had been, not to trust all that God said, and lean on His strength, and so go to their home. Are we like them at all? Let us see.

God says to us, "I will be with you, and lead you on your way. I will take care of you, and keep you, and by and by I will take you to your home. Fear not the toil or the pains of the way; fear not when your foes come near; I am with you; look up to me; when Satan tempts you to sin, and I will drive him off and save you. Fear not when death comes; it is I that have come to take you to your home. Have joy and peace in me; my cloud shall go with you by day, and my fire by night, all through your life. Put your faith in me!"

Do we do so? Or do we, like Israel of old, lose our faith in God as soon as harm comes near? When pain or grief comes to us, do we say, "It is the Lord, let Him do as He thinks best!" or do we cry out with fear, and find fault with God, as Israel did? When sin and Satan tempt us, do we go to God for help to make us good? And when we have done wrong, do we ask Him to blot out our sins for Jesus' sake, and with joy and praise in our hearts bless Him for His dear love, that sent Christ to bear our sins on the cross? Or do we fear, and say, "I am not good, and so I can not come to God." God does not love this, He loves to have us trust in Him. And when we come to die, will we put our hand in God's hand, and say, "O Lord! take us home, Thou dost know the way;" and so have no fear?

If we thus put our trust in God, and walk by His side, it is faith, and it will please Him. But if we have no faith, it grieves Him. How much He did for Israel, and yet they would not trust Him, and so He could not take them to the land of their rest. And so it is with us. We can not go to our Canaan in the skies, if we do not put our trust in God.

Chapter XXV.

THE LONG WAY BACK.

The host of Israel was a long time at Kadesh, just on the edge of the land of Canaan, but at last, sad at heart, they had to take their way back through the wild land.

And now some bad men—Korah, of the tribe of Levi, and Dathan and Abiram of the tribe of Reuben, thought they would like to rule Israel, in the place of Moses. Poor Moses! his heart was so sad for the sin of Israel, that had shut them out of the land of Canaan, that he found it hard to go on, and now these bad men made it still worse.

These men rose up with two hundred and fifty of the chief men of the host, and said to Moses and Aaron, "Ye take too much on you. All the host are God's, each one of them, and the Lord is with them; why do ye then stand so high in the host of the Lord?"

And when Moses heard it, he fell on his face, and told the Lord. Then he said to Korah, "This next day the Lord will show who are His, and will cause him to come near to Him. This do: take cups and put in them the sweet spice that is burnt in the tent of the Lord, and put fire in them, and bring them near to the Lord; and God will show whom He doth choose. Hear, ye sons of Levi! Doth it seem a small thing to you, that the God of

Israel hath set you off from the host, to bring you near to Him, to take care of His house? And do ye seek to be priests, too, in the place of Aaron?"

Then Moses sent to call Dathan and Abiram. But they said, "We will not come; is it a small thing that thou hast brought us up out of the rich land of Egypt, to kill us in these wilds; and now thou wouldst like to be a prince in Israel. Thou dost not bring us to the land of Canaan, or give us fields or homes. Wilt thou put out the eyes of these men? We will not come up."

And Moses was wroth, and said to the Lord, "Judge them, O Lord! for I have done them no harm. I have been just and kind to them."

And he said to Korah, "Come with

your men of Levi to the tent of the Lord, and burn your sweet spice; and Aaron will burn his at the same time."

And they did so, the two hundred and fifty Levites, and stood in the door of the Lord's house in front of all the host of Israel.

And the Lord came down in the cloud in the sight of all Israel, and spake to Moses and Aaron, and said, "Go ye off from this host, that I may kill them at once."

And they fell down, and said, "O God! the God of all souls, shall one man sin, and wilt Thou be wroth with the whole race?"

And the Lord said, "Say to the host, get you up from the tents of Korah, Dathan and Abiram."

And Moses rose up and went to

Dathan and Abiram, and the old men of Israel went him. And he said to the host, "Haste, go far from the tents of these bad men, and touch them not, lest ye die with them."

So they all fled from Korah, Dathan and Abiram; and these men came out and stood in the door of their tents with their wives and all that they had. Oh! how glad they would have been now, if they could have fled from the wrath of God.

And Moses said, "Now shall ye know that the Lord hath sent me; if these men die like all men, then the Lord hath not sent me; but if the Lord make a new thing, and a great pit comes in the ground, and they go down in it, then ye shall know that God's wrath is on them for their sin."

And it came to pass, as he spoke these words, the ground clove at their feet in a great hole, and took in these men and all that was theirs, and they went down in the pit, and were seen no more. And a fire came out from the Lord and burnt up the two hundred and fifty men that burnt the sweet spice in the tent of the Lord.

And all Israel fled in great fear, lest the earth should take them in too.

But the next day they found fault with Moses and Aaron, and said, "Why did ye kill these men?" But while they said this, they saw the cloud of the Lord come down on His house. And Moses and Aaron went near to the Lord, and He said to them, "Go not near the rest of the host, for I have sent a plague on them."

And Moses said to Aaron, "Take fire from the house of the Lord, with the sweet spice; go burn it where the plague is, and pray the Lord to stop it." And Aaron did so, and stood in the midst of the sick to pray; and the Lord heard him, and took from the host the sore plague.

But fourteen thousand died of the plague there.

Then the Lord said to Moses, "Let each tribe take a rod, and write the name of the tribe on it. There will be twelve rods in all; and on the rod of the tribe of Levi write Aaron's name. And put them all in the house of the Lord, and it shall come to pass, that the rod that I shall choose shall bud and bloom. And they did so; and the next day, when Moses went in to look at the rods, lo! the rod of Aaron had buds and bloom and fruit on it. And he brought them all out to show them to the host of Israel.

And the Lord said, "Bring Aaron's rod back to my house, to be kept there as a sign, to show the house of Israel that Aaron and his seed are to be my priests, and no one else must dare to serve in the house of the Lord."

Then the host of Israel came to the wild plain of Zin, and there Miriam died, and they laid her to rest. But it was all dry sand; there were no wells or springs, and once more Israel found fault with Moses and with God, and said, "Would to God we had died when our brothers did! Why have ye brought us here, that we and our flocks should die? Why did ye make us come up out of Egypt, to bring us to this bad place? It is no place of seed, or of figs, or of vines; and we shall die of thirst."

And Moses and Aaron went from them to the door of the house of the Lord, and fell on the ground. And the Lord came to them, and said, "Take the rod, and bring all the host of Israel here, and speak to the rock, and it shall bring forth springs, so that all may drink."

Then Moses took the rod, and brought all Israel to the rock, and he said to them, "Hear, now, ye bad men; must we fetch you springs out of this rock?" He spoke in wrath, and then with his rod he struck the rock twice, when God had told him to speak to it, but had not told him to strike it.

Then the springs came forth, and the men and beasts all drank.

But the Lord spoke to Moses and Aaron, and said, "Ye did wrong; ye did not have faith in me; and now ye shall not bring Israel to the land which I will give them. Ye must die ere they reach that good land, and not go there with them."

What grief must have been in Moses' heart, when he heard the Lord say this! But as it was God's will, he knew it was all right, and he did not ask God to change it. He did not care much for self. He knew God would take care of him. It was for Israel that this good man used to pray, and beg and strive; but as for him, he left the time of his death in the hands of God.

Then Moses sent to the king of Edom, to ask him to let Israel pass through his land, but he would not, so they had to go round it. When they came to Mount Hor, the Lord said to Moses, "Aaron must die here. Take him and his son, and bring them up in the mount, and take the high priest's clothes off from Aaron, and put them on his son." And Moses did so in the sight of all Israel. Aaron died at the top of the mount, and Moses came down with Eleazer, his son, who was to take his place as high priest. Then all Israel did mourn for Aaron thirty days.

So they went on their way; but they would speak hard words of God all the time, and find fault with Him for the long way they had to go. And for this their sin, God sent snakes that bit them so that they died. Then they came to Moses, and said, "We did sin, when we spoke so of God pray to Him to take these snakes from us."

And Moses did pray; and the Lord said, "Make a snake just like these, of brass, and set it on a pole; and it shall come to pass, that all who have been bit, when they look on this, shall live."

And Moses did so; and all who had been bit by the snakes, if they would but look at this snake of brass, got well.

Christ says, "As the snake of brass was put up on the pole by Moses, so hat all who would look at it might live, so shall I be hung on the cross, that all who look to me in faith may live, and not die for their sins."

Then Israel sent word to two kings, Sihon and Og, to ask if they might pass through their land; but they would not let them, and came out to fight with them. And Israel smote them both, and took their lands and their towns; for God was with Israel.

Chapter XXVI.

BALAAM—DEATH OF MOSES.

There was a king whose name was Balak; and when he saw the hosts of Israel come to his land on their way to Canaan, he had great fear, for he thought they would take his land, as they had that of the two kings who would not let them pass through. So he sent for a seer, whose name was Balaam, to come and curse Israel. He thought if this man would curse them, they would fall. He did not know the true God, but put his trust in false gods. So he sent men with gifts of gold and gems, to get Balaam to come and curse Israel.

But God came to Balaam, and said, "Thou shalt not go with them; thou shalt not curse Israel, for they are blest."

So Balaam said to the men, "Go back to your land, for the Lord will not let me go with you." And they went back to Balak, and said, "Balaam will not come."

And Balak sent more men, and more great than they. And they said to Balaam, "The king will make thee a great man, and give thee wealth, if thou wilt go."

But Balaam said, "Stay here this night, and I will ask the Lord what I shall do." Now this was wrong, for God had told him once not to go.

But this night God said to him, "Go; but speak the words that I shall tell thee to speak."

So Balaam rose up the next day, and rode on his ass with the men, to go to Balak. But God sent His angel to stand in the way. And the ass saw the angel, with his sword drawn in his hand, and she went out of the road in fright, and went in the field; and Balaam struck her, to turn her in the way. Then the angel stood in the path, with a wall on each side. And when the ass saw him, she went so close to the wall, that she hurt Balaam's foot; and he struck her once more.

Then the angel went on, and stood in a place where there was no way to turn to the right or to the left. And when the ass saw him, she fell down with Balaam; and he was wroth, and smote her with a staff. And the Lord gave the ass speech, and she said to

Balaam, "What have I done to thee, that thou hast struck me these three times?"

And he said, "Thou didst play a trick on me; I wish I had a sword, and I would kill thee."

And the ass said, "Am I not thine ass, that thou hast used since I was thine? Am I wont to do so to thee?" And he said, "Nay."

Then the Lord did show Balaam the angel who stood in the way, with his sword drawn in his hand; and Balaam fell on the ground for fear.

And the angel said to him, "I went out to stand in thy way, for thou hast not done right. If thine ass had not gone out of the way, I should have slain thee."

And Balaam said, "Shall I go back?"

And the angel said, "No; go on, but speak not one word but what I shall tell thee."

And when Balak, the king, heard that he had come, he went out to meet him, and said, "Why did you not come at first? Do you not know that I can make you a great and rich man?"

And Balaam said, "I have come, but I have not a word to say but what God tells me."

So Balaam did not curse Israel at all, but blest them three times; and Balak did not dare to hurt them.

The time was now come for Moses to die. He had led Israel forty years in the wilds, since God had sent them back from Canaan for want of their faith. All those men had died, and Moses had now brought their sons to the edge of the good land. They were in the plains of Moab, with Jordan's stream in front of them, and the land of Canaan in sight. Yet Moses was not to go in. He said, "O Lord! I pray Thee, let me go in and see the good land."

But the Lord said, "Speak of it no more. It is not best. Go to the top of Mount Pisgah, and lift up thine eyes north, and south, and east, and west, and thou shalt see all the land, but thou canst not go there."

Moses said no more. He was like our Lord Jesus Christ, who said, "Father, not my will, but Thine, be done."

How much we should love this good Moses, if we could see him. And if we go to heaven, we shall see him, for he is there with Christ.

When he knew the day of his death was near, he had all Israel come to him, to hear his last words. He told them all to love their God and keep His laws and did talk to them with great love a long time. He laid his hands on Joshua, and told him to take his place, and lead Israel to Canaan. Then he went with God up to the top of Mount Pisgah, and they saw him no more. God took him, and no man knew where he was laid.

He was a hundred and twenty years old, but his eye was not dim, nor his strength gone. Israel did weep and mourn for him, and well they might, for there has been none in Israel since like Moses, whom the Lord knew face to face.

END OF FIRST SERIES.

www.ingramcontent.com/pod-product-compliance
Lightning Source LLC
LaVergne TN
LVHW022039110826
845151LV00007B/664

* 9 7 8 1 4 2 5 5 3 4 4 5 5 *